VIOLENCE F.C.
West Perth Football Hooligans 1984-86

Kevin Jamieson

Kevin Jamieson attended Mount Pleasant Primary School from 1974-
80 and Applecross Senior High School from 1981-85. Although he
grew up in hardcore East Fremantle territory, he became a West
Perth supporter aged seven in 1976. In May 1984, he co-founded
an unofficial West Perth Cheer Squad, alongside his high-school
friend M.B., which existed up until March 1986. He was an
Accounting Lecturer at Charles Sturt University in 2005-06 but
has been difficult to track down since.

First published in United States of America in 2018 by
LULU PRESS, INC.
627 Davis Drive, Suite 300, Morrisville, NC 27560, U.S.A.
www.lulu.com

Revised Edition © Copyright Kevin Jamieson 2020

Trade paperback, ISBN 978-1-716-66456-4

10 9 8 7 6 5 4 3 2 1

Typeset by Kevin Jamieson

VIOLENCE F.C.
West Perth Football Hooligans 1984-86

Kevin Jamieson

TABLE OF CONTENTS

Table of contents   4

Dedication and acknowledgements   5

Foreword - by Brian Atkinson   6

Chapter 1 - Introduction   7

Chapter 2 - Early Years   16

Chapter 3 - West Perth Cheer Squad 1984   26

Chapter 4 - West Perth Cheer Squad 1985   67

Chapter 5 - West Perth Cheer Squad 1986   85

Postscript   91

References   93

Appendix A - WPFC cheer squad sub-gangs   99

Appendix B - WPFC selected match results   100

Appendix C - Author's WPFC all-stars teams   122

Appendix D - Sandover Medal & WA Footballer of Year   123

Endnotes   126

DEDICATION
For Bradley Potts – those were a good few days.

ACKNOWLEDGEMENTS
I would like to thank: Mr. Brian Atkinson (official historian of the West Perth Football Club and the author of It's a Grand Old Flag); Michael "Mike" Blewett (co-founder of the WPFC Cheer Squad 1984-86); John Devaney of Full Points Footy website and Full Points Publications; Chris Egan (Australian Society for Sports History Perth chapter member, Perth Glory historian, and Peel Thunder supporter); Pave Jusup, Kova, and Sime (senior members of the MCF hooligan firm at Melbourne Knights Soccer Club); Ben McA. (West Perth Cheer Squad member 1984-86); Patrick Mirosevich (present-day South Fremantle Cheer Squad member); Andrew Mulcahy; Mark Whiting (East Fremantle supporter); the contributors to the Lost WAFL Facebook page; and the members of the Say NO to any AFL clubs in the WAFL Facebook group.

DISCLAIMER
The opinions expressed herein are not necessarily the same as those of Brian Atkinson; West Perth Football Club (WPFC); West Perth Football Club cheer squad 1984-86 or any of its members; Swan Districts Football Club (SDFC); Australian Football League (AFL); West Coast Eagles Football Club (WCEFC); Western Australian Football Commission (WAFC); Western Australian Football League (WAFL); and / or any of the people described or mentioned in these pages.

FOREWORD, BY BRIAN ATKINSON

This is a book with a difference. It recounts primarily the memories and reflections of a then 15-year-old school boy who jointly founded a cheer squad for the West Perth Football Club (WPFC) in 1984 to succeed the previous one that was disbanding. These memories and reflections cover the 1984-1986 period. The nature of social relations within the group is also examined.

The author recalls commencing to follow West Perth in 1976 at the age of seven, and describes some of his early memories. The performances of the West Perth team and of many of the players from 1984 to 1986 are then recounted. Readers will enjoy recalling many team and individual highlights from that period in particular. Some interesting exchanges with cheer squads from the other Western Australian Football League (WAFL) clubs are described.

This book will appeal to WAFL traditionalists who mourn the demise of the then elite suburban based tribal football competitions, as they were, within the states. The author expresses some very strong views about the evolution of the national Australian Football League (AFL) competition in 1987, and the impact that the creation of the West Coast Eagles, and subsequently the Fremantle Dockers, had on the WAFL competition. He deplores the corporatization of football. He has similarly strong views on the relocation of the West Perth Football Club from Leederville Oval to Arena Joondalup in 1994. These developments impacted heavily on his enthusiasm for football.

The book will assist to preserve the memories and part of the history of the transition period of the middle- and late-1980s when Australian Rules Football was changed forever, and the impact that this change had on the WAFL.

This book is very well researched, extensively referenced, and very well written. It will create controversy amongst readers. Many will strongly agree with the views of the author. Many will strongly disagree. But all West Perth supporters will enjoy their recollections of the players and the times of the mid-1980s.

Mr. Brian A. Atkinson, West Perth FC official historian, Perth, 19 November 2011.

CHAPTER ONE
INTRODUCTION

"Although Australian Rules is often referred to as 'the people's
game', on account of its broad popularity and appeal, most
writings on the history of football pay insufficient attention
to individual people, and the stories they tell often lack a
human face" (Lionel Frost, Immortals, 2005, p. x).

This book is my memoir, and details my experiences as co-founder
of West Perth Football Club's unofficial cheer squad from 1984
to 1986.1 West Perth (WPFC) is one of the leading clubs in the
Western Australian Football League (WAFL) competition which is
generally regarded today as the third best and most senior
Australian Rules football (hereafter "Australian Rules")
competition in Australia. The book describes the experience of
being a vital member of this 15 to 20-person unofficial grouping
of teenagers aged from 8 years to 18 years which sat behind the
northern or Technical School end of the ground at West Perth's
home stadium, Leederville Oval, from 1984 to 1986. It is an
important part of Western Australian social history as I was
part of the final generation to grow up in the pre-West Coast
Eagles era (I turned 18-years-old in 1986) when the WAFL was
experiencing its glory years. The West Coast Eagles FC joined
the new national competition, known as the "expanded VFL
competition" from 1987-89 and the Australian Football League
(AFL) from 1990 onwards. This event forever changed the position
of the WAFL which was immediately relegated to being a second-
tier league. Average WAFL attendances of around 8,000 per game
in 1986 dropped to around 4,000 per game in the first year of
the expanded VFL competition (1987). Attendances dropped further
still to around 2,000 per game in 1995 when Fremantle Dockers
became Western Australia's second national-league AFL club.
    Although our West Perth group never used physical violence,
and only once was seriously threatened by it (at Bassendean
Oval, the home of Swan Districts Football Club), the football
hooligan academic literature emphasizes the importance of an
"illusion of violence" even when actual violence does not occur.
It defines the hooligan "firm", a class-for-itself to use the
term usually attributed (incorrectly) to Karl Marx, in terms of
a weekly ritual performance of heterosexual masculinity where a
group of hardcore fans defends its physical turf and the honour
of the city and its supporters.
    Australian Rules' cheer squads in the 1980s, when they were
less highly regulated by the leagues and the clubs than they are

today, clearly were involved in this "macho posturing" that Peter Marsh and John Hughson both term an "illusion of violence". This meant physically controlling and protecting the area behind the goals at home games unofficially reserved for hardcore elements of the home team's support and symbolically "invading" the away team's suburban ground. However, in Australian Rules, the cheer squads rarely attempted to take over the home team's area or "end" as was a common practice among British hooligan firms in the 1970s. I believe that, at West Perth, our group would have defended its area behind the goals at the northern end of Leederville Oval if any opposing group of fans had attempted to take it. Given this "macho posturing" and "illusion of violence", I suggest why a group of aboriginal Swan Districts' supporters objected to our cheer squad taking up its prime position behind the goals at the southern-end of Bassendean Oval only 25-metres from where the most dedicated Swans fans congregate in the famous R.A. McDonald Stand.

At grounds like East Fremantle Oval, Fremantle Oval (South Fremantle's ground), and Bassendean, there is no end of the ground that can be regarded as "the away end" meaning the end that is generally neither loved nor patronized by the home fans. (However, at Bassendean Oval, away supporters often congregate in the Bill Walker Stand which is located immediately to the right of the McDonald Stand when viewed from inside the playing arena.) Both ends at those three grounds in the 1980s were effectively occupied, controlled, and monitored by the home fans, making trips to these grounds by semi-organized groups of away fans uncomfortable if not unpleasant. In the period of the cheer squad's existence, we never took an organized group with flags to either East Fremantle or Fremantle Oval and only once did we take a group to Bassendean Oval. One of the reasons behind this was travel cost since most members of our group were working-class teenagers and all but three lived in the West Perth geographic district north of the Swan River centred on Balga, Carine, and Tuart Hill.

Generally speaking, our group's experience conforms to Gary Armstrong and John Hughson's idea of fluid "post-modern" "neo-tribes" where affiliations are very loose and people can easily adjust their degree of commitment to a group and / or leave the group when their personal life circumstances and interests change. Hughson indicates that few people remained integral parts of hooligan firms in the UK beyond their early-20s although Cass Pennant and Rob Silvester's book Rolling with the 6.57 Crew suggests that Millwall's Bushwackers firm probably was an exception in this regard.

As with the UK soccer hooligans, people recognized that joining our cheer squad was totally voluntary, without any of the legal and economic ties that define workplace, marketplace, and institutional relationships. As such, the group members were always careful not to "invade" another member's outside life, i.e. his life outside the group at home, school or work. In this pre-mobile phone and internet era group members rarely contacted each other by phone or met during the week. Group members rarely inquired if someone stopped attending football games. This was not because they did not care but because members recognized that they had no moral authority over another member's life.

Group members only met five times outside match days during the 1984-86 period. Four of these meetings occurred during regular football seasons. Group members met twice on Sundays to attend Channel Seven's "World of Football" programme telecasts held within football club social rooms (once at West Perth and once at Swan Districts); once members met at Perth Football Club at Lathlain Park on a weeknight evening to prepare a banner for the forthcoming state match; and once members attended the Sandover Medal Night in 1984 at the now demolished Perth Entertainment Centre (the only time that the WAFL fairest-and-best player award has been opened to the public). Lastly, on one other occasion, three group members (Mike C., Pete C., and me) went to a season-opening one-day cricket match at the WACA Ground.

When the cheer squad began to break up, in the first few games of 1986, members simply stopped attending games or they attended games but did not sit with the group. No-one made any effort to "go against the grain" and revive or resuscitate the ailing squad. The same thing happened around 1987 at Portsmouth Football Club's 6.57 Crew, as recounted by Pennant and Silvester, when former hooligans found that soccer had lost its appeal and the drug scene became the new object of fashion. Pennant and Silvester state that the prime years of the 6.57 Crew, named after the time that the train carrying fans to away matches left Portsmouth Station, should be regarded as 1981 to 1986. This suggests that the time of the firm's demise can be pinpointed fairly precisely. Nowadays "Pompey" (Portsmouth FC) firm members only get together for commemorative occasions or for major games against rivals such as Millwall or Cardiff.

The West Perth Cheer Squad, I believe, disbanded also as a consequence of new social and occupational divides within the group becoming apparent as well as people's interests changing. For example, I had left school and begun university study; Mark "Thommo" Thompson had left school to become a plasterer; and others had also gone their various ways. I remember talking with Thommo about his plastering work on the Parmelia Hotel job during one Leederville Oval match in 1986 before the cheer squad faded away. I had also drifted apart from school-friend Mike

Blewett as high-school had ended for us in November 1985. He may
not even have returned to the cheer squad for 1986. We became a
little like the punk-band the Clash without Mick Jones! When
group members were all still at school (or most of us), any
social or economic divisions within the group did not seem
important. Group members all bonded together in an egalitarian
atmosphere to support the club and to defend the honour of the
team and the district. Significantly all but three members lived
within the WPFC geographic district and so members could
reasonably think of defending the district and its honour
through the cheer squad.

The cheer squad certainly had a "macho aspect" or an
"illusion of violence". The group was a relatively intimidating
bunch; all of the group members were male (except for the four-
year-old female niece or cousin of the C. brothers); the group
had 15-20 committed members at its peak; and three-quarters of
the group members were aged 14 to 18. In addition to the
committed group of 20, who knew all of the others by name, there
were other people who followed the cheer squad or sat with us
during major games.

At one neutral-venue game, at Subiaco Oval (Round 13 (30
June) 1984 West Perth versus South Fremantle), we joined in with
another West Perth unofficial supporter group, which exists to
this day, known as "Grandstand Falcons" which used to then
congregate at the top of the Leederville grandstand at home
games. At this neutral Subiaco Oval game, our cheer squad sat in
front of the Grandstand Falcons with a third section of seats in
front of the cheer squad reserved for our flags and banners.
Altogether there would have been over 50 people there that day
across both groups combined. The noise the combined group made
under the grandstand roof, on the second- (middle-) tier of the
three-tier stand behind the Fremantle-end goals, was magnificent
when magnified by the echoes. We sang the Grandstand Falcons'
powerful song "This Time (Get It Right)" about England's 1982
World Cup hopes (with England changed to West Perth and the
"white" dropped from "red, white, and blue"). This song summed
up perfectly people's emotions at the time because it had been a
decade since West Perth had last appeared in a grand-final and
hopes had been dashed on several occasions. In hindsight, this
was our cheer squad's greatest day.

This book also considers the cheer squad's chants and songs
(see Chapter 4) as well as the racial or ethnic aspect of
supporting a team commonly known as the "Garlic Munchers", a
name with Italian connotations, which was, during that era, in
the very unusual situation of having a Chinese-Australian player
as captain in the shape of long-serving rover Les Fong (284
games played, 1973-87).

This book also discusses the nature of cheer squad and
ordinary fan support for each of the WAFL teams (Chapters 3-5)
and part of Chapter 4 is devoted to West Perth's on-field
performance from 1984 to 1986. That part-chapter within Chapter
4 also looks at some of the best and most loved West Perth
players of the era. The team had not played in a grand-final
since 1975 but pride in the club meant that, during the period
from 1976 to 1986, West Perth never finished last and in the
1980s it never finished in the bottom two.

I believe that West Perth was driven more by pure confidence
and emotion than some of the other clubs (which were more
clinical and consistent) and, at Leederville Oval during the
cheer squad's era, West Perth was often a formidable team
regardless of the opponent.

A study of the comprehensive statistics section of
Atkinson's It's a Grand Old Flag shows that, in the era between
the premiership in 1975 and the introduction of West Coast
Eagles in 1987 (termed the "drought era" by Atkinson), West
Perth often beat the eventual premier team two or three times a
year during the qualifying rounds. For example, the club
achieved two or three wins a season against Perth in 1977; East
Perth in 1978; Swan Districts in 1982 and 1984; and East
Fremantle in 1985. As such, the club as a whole during the
drought era could be termed an under-performer, although
arguably it never had the true superstars like Cable or Wiley or
Rioli or Mainwaring or Moss or the Krakouer brothers or Hunter
needed to move it from fourth (1985) or third (1982) into second
or first. The cheer squad mirrored the team in spirit. I believe
that the group possessed a larrikin charm, good humour, warmth,
and a good attitude to life. We were all relaxed but committed.
Nearly all group members sat with the group for every game
during its lifetime.

The cheer squad's favourite player was Phil Bradmore (139
games played, 1981-88), a maverick character with long arms and
shaved head (many years before a shaved head became an
obligatory fashion accessory for the over-35s). Bradmore,
restless and wild, each match day used to prowl vast stretches
of territory centring on his centre-half-forward position. The
group members loved his exaggerated gestures and his body
language; his Victorian sophistication (he had played a few
games at Footscray); and his perpetual good-natured teasing
grin. He really looked like he was playing for the camera in an
era when most WAFL matches were not televised. One of the cheer
squad's favourite chants was "Phil Bradmore", followed by the
standard three claps, whenever Bradmore scored a goal or did
anything impressive. Sometimes the chant would break out for no
obvious reason at all. Bradmore affirmed a part of the group

members themselves as the members were mostly mavericks and misfits. Bradmore was an above-average and arguably a brilliant player who was authentic enough to allow his true character and personality to shine through on the field. Brian Atkinson comments as follows about Phil Bradmore:

"I always thought that Phil Bradmore was underrated (so did [1982-84 West Perth coach] Dennis Cometti). I thought he was closer to 'brilliant' than to 'above average'. He was different and 'clowned around' a bit. He played the very difficult position of centre half forward. He was an outstanding mark, a very very good kick, and his accurate creative long handball to players streaming downfield was fantastic. He kicked 193 goals and played in the NSW State of Origin team at the 1988 Australian Football Championships in 1988 in Adelaide. It must have been a good team because it defeated the John Todd coached Western Australian State Team"2

Another of the cheer squad's favourite players was John "Duckie" Duckworth (117 games played, 1977-78, 1981-83, 1985), a strongly-built ruckman or key defender and an ex-Fitzroy (VFL/AFL) player, who missed the 1984 season but made an impressive comeback in 1985 at the age of 35 under new coach John Wynne. Vietnam veteran Duckworth was the physical presence of the West Perth sides of the mid- to late-1970s and the early-1980s. He would bring some strength and machismo into West Perth teams which were badly needed especially during heated encounters with arch-enemy East Perth. Despite his reputation as a tough player, Magarey Medallist Duckworth had a charm, a sense of humour, and a sense of ethics that East Perth's strong-armed players of that era arguably lacked. The "Central District" page at Full Points Footy, a South Australian website authored by football traditionalist John Devaney, writes as follows about John Duckworth:

"Vietnam veteran John Duckworth became Centrals' second Magarey Medallist in 1979 after a barnstorming debut season with the Dogs. Duckworth was the latest in a series of outstanding West Australians to represent the club, and although he only played a total of 42 games over two seasons at Elizabeth his impact on the club as well as on the game in South Australia in general went well beyond this".

The same webpage lists Duckworth as one of the top nine best ever Central District footballers in a list which starts off with the great Hawthorn (VFL/AFL) rover John "The Rat" Platten. Part of this humble, charming, and warm West Perth ethos that

the cheer squad members identified with in the 1980s could be
said to have been a legacy of the West Perth greats of the 1960s
and 1970s, Bill Dempsey, Mel Whinnen, and Graham "Polly" Farmer,
all of whom were fair ball-players and committed team-men who
never wanted to give undue attention to their own efforts. Years
later I would often drive along The Graham Farmer Freeway,
actually a tunnel for most of its length, which follows the same
pathway that Farmer took from East Perth to West Perth, and
silently offer my respects to the great man. Long-serving
players John Duckworth, Les Fong, and Geoff Hendriks (170 games
played, 1975-85) linked the West Perth of the mid-1980s with the
West Perth of the mid-1970s. In the same way, the arrogance and
aggression of former captain Mal Brown lingered on in the East
Perth teams of the late-1970s.

Lastly, most UK soccer hooligans, including Bill Gardner and
Cass Pennant of West Ham United's ICF and Rob Silvester of
Portsmouth's 6.57 Crew, although they regret their involvement
in certain incidents, claim that their years with the firms were
the best of their lives and that overall it was an experience
that they now look back on with extreme fondness. I can say the
same about my time as co-founder of the West Perth unofficial
cheer squad that operated during the years of 1984-86. Brian
Atkinson references this cheer squad as follows: "I certainly
remember the support and enthusiasm coming from behind the
goals, but because it was unofficial nothing was retained on the
record".3

This book aims for a writing style that is accessible to the
wider public but still academically rigorous. It also draws upon
the memories of the other cheer-squad co-founder, Mike Blewett,
based on personal conversations I had with him in Kalgoorlie on
14 July 2011. Mike supplies a key story of the cheer squad's
heated confrontation with the Swan Districts' ruckman-enforcer
of the 1980s Ron Boucher. This is one as yet untold story from
the heated and spiteful clashes between West Perth and Swan
Districts during the 1980s.

As an author I was personally influenced by Nick Hornby's
best-selling autobiographical account of his life as an Arsenal
supporter in Fever Pitch. Hornby's opening section in Fever
Pitch, where he describes the alienation he experienced eating
Monday night dinners in lonely airport hotels with his divorced
father, certainly gives his book an early dose of grim social-
realism and he captures the reader's interest early on. Hornby's
book is a tragic fan's reminisces of life as an Arsenal
supporter. He recounts moving into a home near the Arsenal
soccer ground at Highbury and recalls his disappointment that
the area had moved on and few supporters of the club could be
seen in its streets. He expected men at every house to open

their doors in perfect synchronization at 2.45pm on home match days and then all walk down the footpath together to the ground. In Marxist terms it could be said that Hornby then realized that he had previously "reified" his idealized perceptions of the Finsbury Park district around Highbury by sub-consciously removing the imagined world in his mind from the actual "out-there" reality. The world of the soccer supporters who inhabited Highbury on match days had also become increasingly divorced from the actual life of the surrounding Finsbury Park district.

We also saw these demographic and identity issues arise in West Perth's controversial move to Arena Joondalup from Leederville Oval in 1994 and issues of West Perth's identity have been brought to the forefront of many people's consciousness because of this move. Can you relocate a club and keep its spirit and identity? Can West Ham United's soul survive its 2016 move from Upton Park? The fact that arch-rival East Perth has now taken over the hallowed turf at Leederville Oval is a distasteful fact for some old-time West Perth supporters including me. Mike B. claims that the WPFC has "detached itself from its community"4 because of its relocation to the far northern suburbs which are culturally, socially, and demographically very different from the area around Leederville Oval. West Perth has had a multicultural identity since the Second World War (much like South Fremantle) and its Italian, Greek, and Croatian players and supporters earned it the racist tag of "Garlic Munchers". Can the club keep this multicultural identity after moving to a very-white and very-British area such as Joondalup and surrounds where half the population speaks in an English accent and stickers supporting various lower-division English soccer clubs adorn so many car windows?

I have also been influenced by the books written by West Ham United ICF lead men, Bill Gardner and Cass Pennant; Aberdeen Soccer Casuals' Jay Allan; and Celtic Soccer Crew's John O'Kane. I hope that this book can be seen as having been written in the same spirit, by someone who is both a football fan and an academic researcher.

The chapter of his book Good Afternoon Gentlemen, the Name's Bill Gardner that the lead ICF man Bill Gardner (ably assisted by Cass Pennant) devotes to his favourite West Ham United players over the colourful era of the ICF demonstrates that not all soccer hooligans were stupid people nor did they all lack a genuine interest in the actual games of soccer. As the Amazon customer reviewer of Gardner's book Peter H. Burns writes: "[h]is book exceeds the genre's standards because he actually speaks about the game and its players as much as the aggro that occurred off the pitch. Most of these [other] books have very little to say about the [actual] game at all". Similarly, in

this book many of the great and not-so-great West Perth players
of the mid-1980s are recalled as well as many of the stars from
rival clubs.

CHAPTER TWO
EARLY YEARS

West Perth defeats Subiaco in blinding rain at Leederville Oval
as a seven-year-old watches on

WEST PERTH v SUBIACO
ROUND 11 (19 JUNE) 1976
I began attending West Perth games as a seven-year-old in June
1976. My father L.E.J. first took me to watch the West Perth
home game against Subiaco in June 1976 at Leederville Oval.
Atkinson's statistical section confirms that the date was 19
June 1976 and the final score was: West Perth 14.17 (110)
defeated Subiaco 4.6 (30). My father and I sat directly behind
the fence in front of the tin shed in the north-western corner
of Leederville Oval, only around 20 or 25 metres from where the
cheer squad would congregate for home matches some eight years
later. Neither West Perth nor Subiaco was performing brilliantly
in 1976 although West Perth had won the 1975 premiership and
Subiaco had been premiers in 1973 and finalists in 1974. West
Perth was "won 3 lost 7" prior to the match. It was a day of
shocking weather, blinding rain, and grey sky. Because of this
the official attendance was only 5,346, right at the bottom
level of WAFL home-and-away match attendances in the pre-West
Coast Eagles era. The crowd was sufficiently small that people
could arrive late and sit directly behind the fence. I assume
that the covered seats under the tin shed itself had all been
taken. Although the ground has been re-developed, and West Perth
is no longer based at the ground, the tin shed and the seating
beneath it remains the same today as it was then. Because of the
rain, my father and I left the ground at half-time but the rain
had certainly not dampened my enthusiasm. I remember that I
loved the atmosphere and sense of occasion of league football.
The cheerfulness and brightness of West Perth's red-and-blue
colours appealed to me as the playing jerseys must have stood
out strongly against the grey sky that day.
    I am not completely certain why I chose to support West
Perth in 1976. It may have been due to the media coverage and
hype surrounding the club as a result of the rags-to-riches
fairy tale in 1975 when West Perth, guided by first season
Victorian coach and ex-Fitzroy player Graham Campbell, improved
from last placing in 1974 to premiers in 1975 without, as
Atkinson points out, any new "big name" recruits other than the
inspirational coach. I can certainly remember my father and

grandfather talking about West Perth's surprise successes during the 1975 season over our regular Sunday night roast dinners.

My father L.E.J. had been a casual East Perth supporter from an East Perth family. His uncle-in-law had been a friend of 1955 Perth Football Club premiership player, Hubert "Bert" Wansbrough, who played 127 games for the club between 1952 and 1958. Because of this association, his family would alternate between attending East Perth's home games at Perth Oval and attending Perth's home games at the WACA Ground.5 L.E.J. would irritate his own family of "one-eyed East Perth supporters" by simply "appreciating good football" from something similar to "an umpire's perspective".

My maternal grandfather, Mr. H.A.A. (1906-99), remained a dedicated and devoted Swan Districts supporter right up until his death on 4 July 1999 (aged 93), even though he had moved to Beckenham in the Perth Football Club district as early as 1954. My grandfather used to attend Swans' games weekly, with his best mate Ernie Henderson. They would sit in the R.A. McDonald Stand at Bassendean Oval and in the visiting fans' sections of the grandstands at away games. Their practice was to obtain maximum value for money by being at the grounds for the Colts' games which started around 9.15am or 9.30am. They could then watch three games for the price of one. My grandfather would bring along stacks of sandwiches made by my grandmother Margaret (1910-2003) and value for money was probably the main motivation here as well. Mr. H.A.A. continued to attend games up until around the mid-1980s. My mother6 can remember that when my grandfather was not attending games he would wash his car on the front lawn of the home at 2 Sexton Road, Inglewood whilst listening to the live Saturday afternoon radio broadcasts of the WAFL games. This was 1951-53 and the famous players of the era were Barry Cable, Marcel "Nugget" Hilsz, Bernie Naylor, and Jack Sheedy.

I suppose that I did not want to support Swans (Swan Districts) because I wanted to chart my own course in life. Also West Perth was based reasonably close to my Booragoon home, itself at the eastern end of East Fremantle territory, whereas Swan Districts was based a long way away in the north-eastern outer suburbs close to Guildford and Midland. At my primary-school, Mount Pleasant, during my years there 1974-80, around 80% of football followers supported East Fremantle; 10% or 15% supported East Fremantle's arch-rivals South Fremantle; and 5% to 10% supported one of the other six clubs. There were always some Perth supporters as Perth's local zone bordered East Fremantle's at East Fremantle's zone's eastern extremity the Canning River at South Perth. I can remember being one of only two West Perth supporters at my primary-school. The only other

West Perth supporter in my year was Nigel Barwood. Nigel was not a hardcore supporter by any means but, as was common in the era, he did own the long-sleeved replica playing jersey and he wore it to school. However, as I was well aware, the lack of support for West Perth was due to where I went to school rather than the size of the club's overall supporter base. West Perth still today shares in the second highest WAFL grand-final attendance of 52,322 set in 1975 and the record of 26,760 for a home-and-away game set at a West Perth versus East Perth match at Perth Oval on 31 May 1969. I can say with some assurance that neither of these two figures will ever be beaten now that the WAFL is a second-tier league.

Supporting West Perth built up my resilience and determination during primary-school days. I refused to follow trends or to abandon my team. It was always lonely in a district that was hardcore East Fremantle in those days and if you didn't support the club you had to at least make certain that you respected it. However, I found out that Old Easts was fully worthy of my respect due to its marvellously successful history and its very strong contemporary record against West Perth. I played little-league for East Fremantle versus Subiaco at East Fremantle Oval in 1979 and attended coaching clinics at East Fremantle Oval. For my handball skills I once won a Yellow T-shirt with Selsun Blue on the front (as the shampoo brand was the official sponsor) which resulted in endless primary-school teasing!

I was introduced to the harshness of the real-world in mid-season 1979 when that world invaded the safe, community atmosphere of my primary-school in the form of coach Percy Johnson being sacked mid-season by the WPFC to make way for the return of the prodigal son Graham Campbell who was unable to achieve much success at the club the second time around. At the age of eight I perceived then that it was harsh and unfair for the club leadership to have blamed Johnson for the team's poor performances and of course the club had forgotten that Johnson had led the club to a finals appearance only the previous season.

A staged fight on the footpath on the way to the massive Perth derby at Leederville

WEST PERTH v EAST PERTH
ROUND 21 (26 AUGUST) 1978
My father; an East Perth supporting school friend Tim B.; and I were there for the final home-and-away game of the 1978 season held at Leederville Oval on 26 August 1978. This match attracted a still record Leederville Oval crowd of 24,567 people. I can

remember little of this game except Tim suggesting to me that we stage a mock two-person fight on the footpath on the way from the car to the ground (a stupid idea, as I have always valued authenticity); huge crowds on the large scoreboard bank; and the long time it took waiting in line for ice creams and other food. I also remember that it was a fine warm day more consistent with the coming spring season than of the winter just ending.

West Perth was second before the game whilst East Perth was fifth. A surprise win to East Perth that day, possibly on the back of the vocal support of that club's large army of "fair-weather fans" on the huge scoreboard bank, saw East Perth reach the final-four and West Perth relegated to the first semi-final. The final score was: East Perth 11.19 (85) defeated West Perth 11.10 (76). On the same day, Claremont was defeated by the minor premiers Perth, 15.17 (107) to 15.6 (96), which saw Claremont drop out of the final-four to be replaced by East Perth. This was somewhat ironic for Perth supporters as East Perth then went on to defeat Perth in the grand-final although a young Peter "The Buzz" Bosustow did manage to score a brilliant seven goals for the losers. In the end East Perth was extremely fortunate to defeat Perth by two points on an atrociously wet grand-final day at Subiaco Oval. As Perth's history book From Redlegs to Demons makes clear, Perth played the 1978 grand-final without two of its key players, full-forward Murray Couper and defender John Quartermaine. If these two players had played and / or the day had been fine and / or Barry Cable and Ian Miller had rejoined Perth rather than joined East Perth at the start of the season then surely Perth would have won three premierships in a row to repeat its remarkable feat of the late-1960s.

By 1982 or 1983, when I was in Year 9 and 10 of government high-school (Applecross Senior High School), I gradually stopped going to games with my father who had faithfully taken me to watch West Perth nearly every week of the football season since the Subiaco game in 1976. In Year 10 (1983) I can remember going with classmate and Perth supporter Gaveyn Wood to watch Perth versus West Perth at Lathlain Park. We arrived very early at the game and bought fish-and-chips and a large bottle of Coke from a fish-and-chip shop just outside the city-end of the ground; we consumed these delights seated behind the fence very close to or perhaps directly behind the city-end goals.

In Year 11, the first year of non-compulsory schooling in Western Australia for students turning 16 during the year, I was in a small-sized form class and struck up a friendship with new student, Mike Blewett (hereafter Mike B.), son of a Westpac bank manager, who had spent his life journeying from one city to another including periods living in Brisbane and New Zealand. Mike B. was and is a very interesting character: temperamental, extremely loyal, honest, courageous, cheerful, risk-loving, and full of important and useful insights on life possibly honed during his travels. As at July 2011 Mike was an area supervisor for a building company in Kalgoorlie, effectively operating as principal contractor for jobs in the town. His younger brother, Paul B., also a good friend, is very different personality-wise. He was and is calm, cautious, analytical, and polite. He completed an accounting degree in Queensland and he started work for the Attorney General's Office in Brisbane in 2010.

I met Mike and Paul for the first time in 25 years in September 2009 for an enjoyable afternoon at an Irish pub at Surfers' Paradise on the Gold Coast. Neither had changed much. Mike spent the lunch ensconced behind his dark sunglasses and he preferred to stand rather than sit. Typical of his generosity he willingly and spontaneously shouted me lunch and several pints of Kilkenny. Paul was wearing a Fremantle Dockers AFL polo shirt, something that is rarely seen in Queensland. A picture on the WAFL Golden Era website shows Mike B. (left) and me at the Exchange Hotel, Kalgoorlie, Western Australia on 14 July 2011.

During 1984, my friendship with Mike B. grew and he was also part of a friendship group centred on Len Shearer Reserve in Booragoon. During 1984 and 1985, I came to belong to three informal friendship groups: a school one, a neighbourhood one, and our West Perth cheer squad. These three groups had no common elements in terms of people involved other than the fact that Mike B. and I were part of all three groups. The neighbourhood group had an average age two or three years younger than the school group although it included two friends one or two years older than me, namely Peter "Pete" Lansbury (a hardcore East Perth supporter) and Leon D'Alton. Some of the younger people included Paul Blewett, Cathy Bray, Cesare Ceniviva, Bobbie Jenkins, Gary Laing, Julian Leach, Todd Pedler, Andrew Ross, Glen "Swifty" Swift, Mick and Stuart Van Duren, and Carl Wykes. We would hold impromptu Australian Rules football and soccer games at Len Shearer Reserve after-school and in school-holidays and some of these games became fight-to-the-death, brutal affairs of four-against-four or six-against-six. Games usually ended when it was too dark to see the ball. May school-holidays were characterized by warm sunny days and chilly mornings so for most of the day people had jumpers tied around waists.

Another young rebel who was around the place at the time was Gary O'Loughlin who had set in motion an East Fremantle Cheer Squad. This group (joined by me on one or two occasions as a source of moral support for Gary) had around ten members but I can't say for how many seasons it existed for. The legendary high-school Wild Man Jason Hadden was a part of this group or at least could sometimes be observed within the group's vicinity at

East Fremantle home games and at Fremantle derbies. Jason had a strange habit of sometimes hiding under staircases at high-school and then jumping out at people.

Another time Greg Kinnane and I were in the front section of Garden City Shopping Centre around 6pm, that twilight time when the shops have closed and straggling shoppers are moving at glacial pace towards the exits. There was a big central display area featuring large wine bottles and no type of security protection right in the middle of the front section where the east-west mall intersects with the north-south mall. With Greg in the lead, we took a bottle of wine each and started sprinting full-pace northwards down the section of mall leading up towards Myer and Timezone. From around 50 metres behind us a security guard shouted out for us to stop. Following Greg's lead again, we placed the bottles on the ground whilst still at full-speed (like touching the ball to the ground on a long run in Australian Rules football) and kept going, before finally turning left and exiting the shopping centre next to Timezone. The security guard did not bother to continue his chase after the wine bottles had been surrendered so Greg was correct in his assessment of what the guard's psychology would be. We were on a high of adrenaline afterwards and exhausted from some serious sprinting effort over around 250 to 300 metres.

During first term of Year 12 in 1985, from late January through to the May school holidays, there used to be occasional huge parties at Shirley Strickland Reserve in Ardross on Saturday nights. These parties could attract 100 to 200 people which were remarkable numbers for the pre-social media era. Most people were Year 12s, although there were younger high-school students present, and the beverage of choice was pre-mixed drinks cans. I was familiar with Shirley Strickland Reserve as it was the home ground for the Mount Pleasant Junior Football Club (the Mounties) and was sometimes used by Mount Pleasant Primary School for intra-school games. Because these parties were so huge, sometimes you could meet and chat with younger people whom you might not have talked to for years. I can remember once talking with Ashley Burton who had been a year below me at Mount Pleasant Primary School and had played and trained with me on that same oval for the Mounties three or more years before. My last year with Mount Pleasant JFC had been Under-14s in 1982 under the coaching of Craig "Craigo" Campbell. The bonds of primary-school and junior football tended to stay strong over the years and those more carefree days were looked back upon fondly. Territorial concepts established in primary-school days continued on to high-school so we felt a continuing connection with our local territory east of Riseley Street; north of the Brentwood shops at Cranford Avenue; south of around

Gibson Street; and west of the Canning River. Similarly, we felt the same continuing connection with the people whom we had gone to primary-school with and these people for the most part still lived in this area. The area occupied by our high-school and the catchment zones of neighbouring primary-schools were always regarded as being foreign territory and I don't think bonds were ever as deep with people from these more distant areas. However, my affection for and closeness with our friendship group centred on Len Shearer Reserve, in the new part of Booragoon west of Riseley Street, would appear to cast some doubt upon any mechanistic application of this theory.

My first kiss was at one of these parties. I can't recall the girl's name but she was English and she was one year below me at school. I think she was somehow connected with Jonathon May, Nicholas Edwards, John Henderson, and Scott Laing's British gang (our very own Glasgow Rangers). The location of the event was where a second-slip or gully fieldsman might be standing for a left-hand batsman and a fast bowler coming in from the southern end. As there was an artificial cricket pitch at the centre of the ground this place was easy to identify even in the middle of the night and a vast distance from the street-lights.

Once at Shirley Strickland Reserve, some years before during a Mount Pleasant Primary School intra-school game, I was playing on the wing on the western side of the ground. The umpire Mr. Alan Burrough was about to throw the ball up in the centre of the ground to re-start play. His back was turned and, as he heard me speak out negatively about the umpiring standards (!), he turned around in an instant, pointing at me and shouting "You, off!" After I walked off the field I soon realized that no-one was paying any attention to me anymore. Realizing this, I left the oval and walked east along Coogee Road; south along Bedford Road; east along Queen's Road; and then south along Henley Road back to the primary-school. By this time it was around normal going-home time (3.20pm) and I got into Mum's waiting car, as normal, and we drove away. No mention was ever made at school about this day's events. I was a little apprehensive at school the next morning but, as time passed, I realized that there would be no adverse repercussions. Did Mr. Burrough forget about the incident or did he just decide to put it to rest? There was another teacher at our primary-school around this time, Mr. Garry Jones. I once approached him for an autograph in the school-grounds one lunch-time, because he had played 28 WAFL games for Perth Demons, but he just laughed in my face along with his mate Mr. Ronald "Ron" Dunsire.

On the night before the final day of school in Year 12 in 1985, a large group of people, led by Gordon H., a Rangers FC supporter from Glasgow and some others, arranged to meet outside

the school grounds at 2am or 3am. The prank plan was to dig out
a youthful tree and plant it again inside the locked part of the
high-school compound. When I arrived on foot, wearing my new
mail-order Iron Maiden Trooper T-shirt, the outside digging-up
operation had already begun. The crowd was large so I was five
metres away or more from the action with a partially obscured
view. The night cannot have been too cold as I was wearing only
a T-shirt. The digging up must have been a harder task then
anticipated; and it took ages. After a certain amount of time
with limited action I turned around and walked back home before
dawn rose. I think the overall plan was not a failure as it was
possible to get inside the locked-up part of the school compound
because a teacher had given Gordon the key. For years I had
lived with the thought that Gordon H. had suicided not long
after high-school ended but he was "found" on Facebook several
years ago safe and living in England. Mike B. had to admit that
his information had been wrong this time around.

In the 1985-86 cricket season (or possibly the 1984-85
season), I joined as wicketkeeper for Applecross Under-16s when
Gordon was the number one express bowler; he was quick but his
bark was worse than his bite. He was a certainly a fearsome
sight for the batsmen as he stormed in off his long-run while he
was an interesting and fascinating sight for me as wicketkeeper
stationed a large distance back from the stumps. Our home ground
was Heathcote Reserve near the then still-functioning lunatic
asylum.7 I caught a catch off a no-ball in the first over of my
first match which reinforced people's prior hopes that I could
do the job. I did get one legitimate caught-behind down the leg-
side in this first match. I do regret not continuing with my
cricket career after this season. One especially enjoyable part
of the wicketkeeper's job, as I found out, is the continual
chats which take place with the slips fieldsmen standing next to
you which usually include the team's captain.

My favourite bands from 1984 to 1986 were AC/DC, Deep
Purple, Iron Maiden, Judas Priest, Led Zeppelin, Metallica,
Rainbow, Saxon, and Scorpions. I loved the "New Wave of British
Heavy Metal" (NWOBHM) movement, which I now understand to have
been an exciting synthesis of punk and traditional heavy-metal.
I can recall listening to a heavy-metal Monday night weekly
radio program, probably in 1985 but perhaps 1986, and hearing
Metallica's "Fight Fire with Fire", "Hit the Lights",
"Motorbreath", "Creeping Death", and "Whiplash", all songs from
the band's first two albums Kill Em All (1983) and Ride the
Lightning (1984). I can remember being completely stunned as I
had never heard music played that fast. One memory I have is of
catching the Number 105 bus after school to go to visit the
heavy-metal shop Twilight Records in Perth city-centre and

talking to Mitchell Duke on the bus journey. He had been a year
behind me at my primary-school. I did not know him well at all,
but we began talking and I soon discovered that he was a heavy-
metal fan who also loved Judas Priest. I also remember sitting
on the Mount Pleasant Primary School Oval on New Year's Eve 1985
with Glen "Swifty" Swift (from the new section of Booragoon) and
singing "Two Minutes to Midnight" by Iron Maiden whilst drinking
beer. Only I was singing as Swifty was not a heavy-metal fan! He
was impressionable and about three years younger than me which
explains why he was laughing at the gruesome song lyrics.

From Attadale to Mumbai

SCHOOL-HOLIDAYS
AUGUST 1985
In the May or August school holidays of 1985 (probably August) I
spent some time with Bradley Potts, who was then in Year 9 and
was the adopted younger brother of Shari (who had been in my
year in primary-school). Bradley was tall and broad-shouldered
for his age (around fourteen) with a real presence, quiet self-
confidence, charisma, and a good sense of humour. He had thick
medium-brown hair which flopped over to one side on his
forehead.

Bradley knew these two girls of the same age as him. Maryann
McKenna went to Applecross while the Indian girl, Maryann's
close friend, went to Santa Maria Roman Catholic College. For a
few days in a row we all hung out all day at the Indian girl's
huge double-storey mansion on the riverside at 238 Burke Drive,
Attadale 6156. Her mother was the real-estate agent Sue
Moncrieff (who still works in the Attadale area today in the
same capacity). No adult was at home during the day-time so the
four of us were there by ourselves each day. It was very
relaxing and fun, with good company, in a very luxurious
environment. We would swim in the pool, unwind on the balcony,
and drink the Moncrieff family's Bailey's Irish Cream (or some
similar hard-liquor).

Days were warm and sunny and extremely enjoyable. For a few
days in a row, I would cycle direct to the Moncrieff house in
the mornings and leave late in the afternoons. For those days it
was always the same four of us. The days seemed to go on forever
but soon we were back in school and I never saw that beautiful
Indian girl (Sharima) any more although I would think about her
from time to time as the years passed.

I dropped out of regular contact with Bradley after school
re-started. In a government high-school of one thousand
students, by the time you reached Years 11 and 12, you knew so
many people that you would drift from group to group and from

person to person. It partly depended on who you bumped into at school during break-times and in the streets, shopping centres, and parks of the surrounding heartland areas. I heard later on that Bradley committed suicide (?) and this came as a shock to me as I remember his cheerfulness, shy bravado, self-confidence, and good humour. Perhaps his adoption raised issues and his sincerity and low-key charm perhaps were better suited to humbler working-class districts than to aspirational and self-centred Applecross/ Mount Pleasant. Sometimes I would later think that, if I had kept up the friendship with Bradley (and the informal mentoring which the age gap encouraged), then his future might have turned out to be different.

Bradley's school-friend from his early days at high-school, Andrew Mulcahy, has this to say about him:

"I remember him as an alpha male with a troubled past but a sense of adventure. He loved to push the boundaries and act ten years older than his age. He was funny as fuck and a true larrikin, street-wise and able to look after himself and his mates. His dad was an alcoholic and his mum was super-sweet. His sister was a quiet girl and he was, like his sister, adopted. I'm sure they lived in a house in St. Michael's Terrace [Mount Pleasant] which was state-housing. … Pottsy left home by the age of 15".8

Andrew also has some good memories of times spent at the Moncrieff's house as a 13-year-old around this time (1985): "The house was on Burke Drive. I remember jumping off the second-level into the pool and VB cans and Peter Jackson fags!" Then Andrew says: "I dated Sharima. We used to walk over the road and get some random person to buy us the piss. I nearly died there a few times [jumping into the pool]: Thirteen-years-old and bullet-proof, or just fucking lucky".

On 18th-19th April 2018, I had a vivid dream where I was in Mumbai, India and, unsurprisingly, the dream was full of Indian people. However, because I had never been to India, the district resembled an exclusive, up-market, residential suburb of Perth with big, modern housing (such as Woodvale or Ocean Reef but with larger lots). I looked across to one huge, fantastic, modern house set in a large, flat, grassed lot and, somehow in the dream, I believed or I knew or I told myself that this was where the Moncrieff family had moved to. I guess, so many years later, I was still searching for that beautiful 14-year-old Indian girl I had spent a few days with so many long years ago. It was a magical few days, so unexpected when it happened but part of the possibilities which the late-teenage years always promise, that could never be repeated.

CHAPTER THREE
WEST PERTH CHEER SQUAD: 1984

This chapter takes readers directly on to the formation of the West Perth Cheer Squad in the first half of the 1984 WAFL home-and-away season. Following this, this chapter introduces each one of the core cheer squad members individually and discusses the norms of social relationships within the group.

Sooner or later, during the first half of 1984, Mike B. declared his hand as a West Perth supporter, and I was and am tremendously happy about this. Without Mike B. it is very doubtful whether the cheer squad could ever have happened or been successful. At that time I did not know whether Mike had simply decided to follow my team or whether he had had an earlier attachment to West Perth. In 2011 Mike told me that he had followed his father to support West Perth when he still lived in Perth city in the period up to his turning five-years-old.9

I had become aware, early in the 1984 season, that the earlier famed West Perth Football Club cheer squad, which had congregated behind the northern-end goals at Leederville for many years, had quit completely at the end of 1983. This cheer squad was interesting as, unlike most cheer squads in Australian Rules' history in Victoria, South Australia, and Western Australia, it was dominated by middle-aged females and young children. The legendary leader of this group was a woman known by the woefully politically incorrect moniker of "Fat Pam" (real name: Pam Hynsen). The leading women used to stand upright on the last row of wooden benches behind the northern goals thus placing considerable strain upon the said benches. Their cheer squad was large, committed, and dedicated; it had a huge collection of flags and floggers. This group had operated for a number of years and was well known and respected. I sat near the group at the northern-end of East Fremantle Oval for an East Fremantle versus West Perth match in Round 17 (8 August) 1981.10

East Fremantle Oval, where the aloof hostility and relentless force of the home team and home crowd are matched only by the winds blowing in from the Indian Ocean only a few kilometres away, has always been regarded as a remote and inhospitable place. It was (and is) the most difficult traditional WAFL ground to reach by public transport as it does not have a nearby train service. People were required to either take the low-profile local suburban bus services (numbers 146 and 154 in the 1980s) up Marmion Street from Fremantle or the high-frequency flagship 106 route along Canning Highway from either Perth or Fremantle. Taking the 106 meant walking from

Canning Highway through vaguely hostile back-streets to the northern corner of the ground where one was met by barb-wire fencing and the rear of a tin shed. A trip there during the 1980s was the local WAFL equivalent of journeying to Millwall Football Club's famous Den ground in south-east London.

Given East Fremantle's great success, as the club with the most premierships won in the WAFL11 (West Perth is second12), a trip to East Fremantle Oval usually meant a resounding defeat at the hands of the home team. East Fremantle had and has an amazing culture of success, whereby anything less than a grand-final appearance is viewed as a disappointment and a bottom-four finish is simply beyond the pale, the end of the world, and totally unacceptable. As an example, East Fremantle's history book comments about the 1975 season as follows: "What went wrong?" The author Jack Lee cites the club's magazine Scoreboard which stated: "All sorts of excuses will be put forward for our failures in 1975, but the simple truth lies in the simple statement that we just weren't good enough". However, this "failure" was actually a season when the club won 10 games, lost 11, and finished fifth out of eight clubs. Such a result would not have been considered a major failure at some other WAFL clubs including perhaps West Perth which often finished fifth or sixth during its premiership "drought era". Full Points Footy's John Devaney comments indirectly on the East Fremantle winning culture in the following passage:

"As far as on-field performances go, the twenty-first century has, to date, been far from auspicious, with the club failing to qualify for the finals every season between 2003 and 2009, and even succumbing to the rare, if not quite unique, indignity of wooden spoons in 2004 and 2006. Restoring the club to what many would argue is its rightful place at the forefront of the West Australian game is going to be far from easy, but the [East Fremantle] Sharks have faced stiffer challenges over the years, and triumphed, and it would surprise no one to see them challenging seriously for premierships again within the next two or three seasons".

However, Brian Atkinson correctly points out that:

"[T]o balance East Fremantle's great successes in the 20th century, perhaps reference should be made to their disastrous start to the 21st century. In the first 11 seasons of the 21st century from 2001 to 2011, East Fremantle have only made the finals twice, 4th in 2002, and 3rd in 2010. They have finished 9th (last) twice, 8th once, and 7th three times".13

The only other Australian Rules club in Australia with a similar long-term winning culture to East Fremantle is the club John Devaney has supported since childhood, Port Adelaide Magpies in the SANFL. How the East Fremantle winning culture gets retained and transmitted from one generation to the next, especially in these days of the WAFL as a feeder-league with a high regular turnover of players, is itself amazing. Nearly all football followers in Perth, including me, have total respect for East Fremantle, its successes, its culture, its sheer force and (long term, historical) dominance, and its complete professionalism. For Fat Pam's West Perth cheer squad to take such a large and organized group with flags and floggers to East Fremantle Oval in August 1981 is also worthy of tremendous respect. This is especially so given that this match was between fifth (WPFC) and seventh (EFFC) on the ladder and West Perth was four premiership points outside the top-four before the game. As it was West Perth only one won more game for the season and finished in sixth position with 8 wins and 13 losses (percentage 77.3%).

However, with Fat Pam's cheer squad disbanded, I sensed a gap and an opportunity. As far as I was aware, in May 1984, Fat Pam's group continued to make the banners that the players ran through at the start of each game (they may still make these banners today), and our group never attempted to get involved in this activity, mostly out of respect for Fat Pam's group which had been there long before it. Furthermore, banner making is complicated and tiresome work and I doubt whether our group in 1984 would have had the patience for it. The northern-end at Leederville Oval in 1984 was strangely quiet, empty, and barren, now devoid of West Perth flags and floggers on home match days. I felt that the team would be inspired by a vocal group of home supporters, with a colourful red-and-blue visual presence, at the northern-end of Leederville. A Melbourne Knights' soccer supporter puts forward her view (below) that her team has been inspired and encouraged on occasion by the vociferous, noisy, and colourful support of the club's hooligan firm Melbourne Croatia Fans or MCF:

"From what I can gather, the MCF is largely made up of young men who are passionate about their club, its heritage and its importance to the Croatian community. They are loyally devoted to their team and will often travel great distances in order to show their support. The songs, chants and banners have (according to the players) been known to lift our team in crucial moments during the match".14

My personal notes from the 1984 season state that I attended two of the first five West Perth games before the formation of the cheer squad. I was inspired to set up a new unofficial cheer squad to replace Fat Pam's group behind the northern-end goals at home matches and to travel to select away games. I expected that the demographics of my new group would be totally different to Fat Pam's group but I hoped that our members would show the same loyalty, dedication, commitment, and spirit. The new cheer squad would have a lot to live up to.

Being somewhat naive about the ways of the world, and then aged 15, I placed an advertisement in the "Public Notices" in the "Classifieds" section of our daily newspaper, The West Australian, to appear one Friday in May 1984, the second full month of the new football season. The advertisement asked any individuals interested in forming a new West Perth cheer squad to meet at the next home game and to look for the flags. Of course teenaged football supporter are unlikely to be consulting such an obscure section of the newspaper's Classifieds every day of the week just waiting for such an ad to appear!

I recently located this ad in the microfilm copies of The West Australian held at the Battye Library in Perth. The ad appeared on p. 41 of The West Australian on Friday 4 May 1984, directly below the opening ad for the "Public Notices" section "Acrylic nails beautiful hands for just $25". My ad read as follows: "ANYONE interested in being part of a West Perth football cheer squad pref age 11-17 meet at the ground this Saturday. Look for the flags". There are several coded messages for insiders here with the name of the football ground for the next day's game not being mentioned on the assumption that fans dedicated enough to join a new cheer squad would know where the game was to be played. It puts the onus on the reader to "look for the flags", rather than specifying an exact location, perhaps because Mike B. and I had not decided beforehand where to congregate. The ad assumes that the reference to "West Perth" would be enough to communicate to insiders that it is the WAFL club being referred to and not a more minor club in another football code such as the then West Perth Macedonia (now Stirling Lions) Soccer Club. The preferred ages listed (11-17) are typical of cheer squads for the era, based on the Victorian and South Australian models, and most of the group's members did turn out to be within this age range. Including the ad in the Friday rather than the Saturday edition was perhaps my attempt to communicate to readers that this cheer squad was to be treated as serious, "week-day" business although it would meet on Saturdays. I am surprised that I did not put the ad in the Business section!

Ronnie Davis helps secure the draw in the dying minutes at Leederville

WEST PERTH v SOUTH FREMANTLE
ROUND 6 (5 MAY) 1984
As mentioned, Mike B. was willing and interested in the cheer squad idea so, together on the Saturday 5 May 1984, the day subsequent to the Friday of the advertisement, Mike B. and I took the Number 105 bus from Booragoon into Perth city-centre, walked two blocks from St George's Terrace to Barrack Street (just north of Murray Street), and then caught the 1.15pm Number 15 bus to Glendalough. Mike B. and I then alighted near the ground along the Oxford Street cappuccino strip, not far from the corner with Vincent Street. I am fairly sure that Mike B. and I already had two large red-and-blue homemade flags on this day. The ad did clearly say "look for the flags". The group would add significantly to these two flags over the next two years ending up with around 15 flags at one point or approximately one flag per core member. On this day Mike B. and I both wore long-sleeved West Perth replica playing jerseys. Although these were not the height of fashion even in the mid-1980s Mike B. and I were both very proud to show off our club loyalties.

Contemporaneous newspaper reportage confirms that this match was the thrilling home draw against South Fremantle on 5 May 1984 described by Atkinson in his book It's a Grand Old Flag. Atkinson recounts that the slender Aboriginal forward flanker Ron "Ronnie" Davis kicked two goals out of three for West Perth in the last five minutes to draw the game with only fifteen seconds remaining.15 The final score was: West Perth 15.15 (105) drew South Fremantle 16.9 (105) and the official attendance was 7,790. I certainly do remember a joyous mood that day commensurate with an exciting come-from-behind draw. It was the perfect on-field start to begin the cheer squad era! I also remember that the weather was fine but cold. It was the first drawn match in the WAFL since 20 April 1974. It is remarkable that the games I now classify as the first and last games for the cheer squad were both draws, versus South Fremantle at Leederville Oval on 5 May 1984 and versus Perth at Lathlain Park on 29 March 1986.

Mike B. and I must have exerted an aura of charm and authenticity on this day as a number of people came up to us, introduced themselves, and stayed with us for the rest of the afternoon including Courtney; Rohan H.; and Mark T. (hereafter "Thommo"). Some of these people, including the three names mentioned, would become core members of the cheer squad and stick with the group for the next two years. I think that people were aware that Fat Pam's long-serving cheer squad had withdrawn from active service at the northern-end goals at the end of 1983, and some people may have been waiting or hoping for a new group to form (whether connected to the previous group or otherwise).

If my memory serves me correctly, Courtney and his friend Rohan H. both joined the group on the first day. Both were to form part of the core for the next two years with Courtney arguably filling a role as deputy leader, along a second rank, with his suburban junior football friend Thommo who most probably joined the group on that first day as well. In our group there were tiny sub-gangs following the same pattern, but with smaller numbers, as Sheffield United's Blades; Portsmouth's 6.57 Crew; or the Peruvian barras bravas of Lima. The sub-gangs operated along the lines of friendships formed prior to joining the group and suburbs of residence. The sub-groups had two or three people in each, and each sub-group had a particular relationship with the joint-founders, Mike B. and me, and with the group as a whole. Appendix A lists the sub-gangs and the members belonging to each. Courtney and Rohan (the "Carine group") was a sub-gang, as was the "Balga group" of Peter "P.A." Brennan (family name changed) and Rex Tong (name changed). Thommo and Robbie, who joined the cheer squad only in 1985, were viewed as "floaters" or non-aligned.

Because Thommo and Robbie knew each other and Thommo knew Courtney prior to anyone joining the group they were key links between the sub-gangs. People from the same district were viewed as sub-gangs since they would habitually take the same buses or trains to and from the games together. It was possible to see a very shaky organizational chart emerge of the core since the two blonds, Courtney and Mike B., had always had a strong relationship, while I related reasonably well with the red-haired Thommo. The cheer squad also included the three Coughlan brothers (aged 14, 15, and 16 at the group's inception) (hereafter the C. brothers) who had spent considerable time in reform homes and were commonly perceived as having no fixed abode.

As with the Sheffield United Blades members, studied by Armstrong, the core cheer squad members were all dedicated West Perth supporters and the core members regarded the group as important in their lives and in their match-day experiences of fandom. The core group members were all "traditional" and "hot" supporters based on Richard Giulianotti's theory of the four types of soccer spectators in the global game, namely "supporters" (traditional, hot); "followers" (traditional, cool); "fans" (consumerist, hot); and "flâneurs" (consumerist, cool). Although Mike B., Courtney, and Rohan engaged in conspicuous consumption in the area of fashionable dressing this consumption did not extend to their football support which remained "traditional" and "hot". Group members who only occasionally attended games, such as Robert C., might be classified as followers with "traditional" yet "cool" forms of club identification.

The group members took advantage of people's natural good connections and natural feelings for one another; the group founders worked on strategically building and making full use of these relationships. On the other hand, if two people did not relate very well or easily, this weak link in the chain was bypassed with these two people largely avoiding each other but each one building strong relationships with other core members. Prickly relationships were subtly monitored by the core members to make sure that they were kept manageable and within reasonable limits. It was understood that the general will of the cheer squad was more important than anyone's private agenda. The cheer squad members understood, even from day one, that if key relationships were not kept harmonious then people would not be attracted to the group. Group members realized that an atmosphere of warm camaraderie and good humour, as well as a somewhat "macho" atmosphere, were necessary for the cheer squad to thrive and grow. This atmosphere was both authentic and had to be consciously worked at each match-day.

Although the group, sadly, did not grow much over its two-year life, the core 15-20 members were loyal and dedicated, and, on good days of fine weather and interesting opponents, large numbers of hangers-on and drifters of various ages would join us. This was especially so at away games where West Perth fans had no habitual place(s) to sit and were wary of the home team supporters. This is why club colours were important so, other than Mike B., Courtney, and Rohan, group members did not follow the designer dressing style of the 1980s English soccer "casuals". West Perth fans, especially at away games, would tend to look for and congregate with groups of people wearing the club colours and looking like an authentic and believable gang of supporters. During the 2013 WAFL season, I noticed travelling Perth Football Club supporters congregating together in certain corners of the ground at both Bassendean and Claremont Ovals. Our West Perth Cheer Squad was also very fortunate that there were many fine-weather Saturday afternoons in 1984 which kept group attendances and people's enthusiasm for the group high.

My personal 1984 season notes, compiled during 1984, state that Mike B. and I did not attend the next three games, Swan Districts versus West Perth at Bassendean Oval (12 May); West Perth versus Perth at Subiaco Oval (19 May); and Subiaco versus

West Perth at Subiaco Oval (26 May), because I was on holiday in Adelaide and Melbourne. I attended the next game, West Perth versus East Perth at Leederville Oval (Monday 4 June) with school-friend Roy "The Spoon" George and the cheer squad may or may not have been in action that day. It took some weeks for the cheer squad to gel and solidify, and to grow to the structure and size that it had during the 1985 season.

Fourteen-year-old Courtney was a designer dresser in the manner of the English "soccer casuals" of the 1980s. He was very interested in fashion. I think that he also had a long-sleeved West Perth replica jersey but, other than that somewhat unfashionable item of clothing, he always wore colourful vee-neck woollen jumpers (pullovers); bulky cargo shorts (even on the coldest days); and navy deck shoes without socks. Courtney came from a middle-class or upper middle-class family suburb in WPFC's geographic district. It was most likely Carine which is today part of Subiaco's recruiting zone. In my memory I had thought that Courtney's family name was Walsh, but this seems unlikely given that "Courtney Walsh" was the name of a famous West Indian cricketer of the era. Courtney Jones is another possibility.

Brown-haired, 14-year-old Rohan Hollicks was a slender, quiet lad who stuck close to Courtney. They were school-friends in the northern suburbs and both were committed to the group from the first match. I can say that I never got to know Rohan well. His manner was aloof and unapproachable, but this was not due to arrogance; more likely it was because of shyness and caution. Rohan was very much an introvert but he showed his commitment to the group by his regular attendance for two years. Courtney and Rohan were together the "middle-class" and the relatively more self-controlled sub-gang within the core but they also enjoyed the more boisterous and insulting chants and songs. If you could say that there was a second layer of leadership, "below" Mike B. and me, it would have been the trio of 14-year-olds Courtney, Rohan, and Thommo. Nobody could dare to think that there might have been a third layer but the prepubescent sub-gang ("Half", "Thommo Junior", and Mario) clearly ranked lower in sub-cultural prestige than all of the others in the core, but still higher than people in the periphery whom group members did not know personally. Of course the sub-gangs of Mike C.-Pete C. and P.A.-Rex Tong might have viewed themselves as second- or third-tier leaders, and such claims would have been more than plausible.

Brothers Mike Coughlan (16-years-old) and Pete Coughlan (14-years-old) were also key members of the core group for part of 1984 and all of 1985. These brothers were different in temperament in the same manner as the B. boys were, with the elder one being volatile and the younger one being calm and collected. They had been in and out of reform homes all their lives. If Courtney and Rohan was the "middle-class" sub-gang then the C. brothers were the "lumpenproletariat" or "dangerous classes" (to use the two terms of Karl Marx). Academic hooligan literature from England and many European countries suggests that hooligans are mostly working-class although the percentage in professional and managerial occupations was stable and increasing. The working-class dominance is not apparently the case in Italy or in some South American locations where it is more middle-class based.

Generally speaking the West Perth Cheer Squad conforms to the idea of fluid "post-modern" "neo-tribes" where affiliations are very loose and people can easily adjust their degrees of commitment to a group and / or leave the group when their personal priorities and interests change. Hughson indicates that few people remained integral parts of hooligan firms in the UK beyond their early-20s although Cass Pennant and Rob Silvester suggest that Millwall's Bushwackers firm was probably an exception. Armstrong writes that by the 1980s the "vast majority of Blades were aged between seventeen and twenty-eight". As with the UK soccer hooligans, people recognized that joining the West Perth Cheer Squad was totally voluntary, without any of the legal and economic ties that define workplace, marketplace, and institutional relationships. As such, the group was always careful not to "invade" another member's outside life, i.e. his life outside the group at home, school or work. Group members rarely contacted each other by telephone or met during the week outside of Saturday match-days. Group members only met five times outside of match days during the whole 1984-86 period and only once outside of football season (when Pete C., Mike C., and I attended a season-opening one-day domestic cricket match at the WACA Ground).

Regardless of his background, everyone in the cheer squad was treated and valued equally, and I believe that each group member experienced and enjoyed the camaraderie of the group. Without these positive factors each individual in the core would not have stuck with the cheer squad for two years when there were no legal, economic or moral ties to bind anyone to the group. People had to enjoy sitting with the group or the group would lose them. Everyone made the effort to create a warm and cheerful atmosphere; to welcome newcomers; and to encourage each other amidst the usual teasing and insults that you might expect in the male group situation. Everyone certainly was a dedicated West Perth supporter and the core members regarded the group as important in their lives and vital in their match-day experiences of fandom. No-one in the group was like those

English soccer hooligans whom, allegedly, are not interested in the actual game or their club. The founders felt responsible for providing the group with a minimum of organization; making sure that teasing and insults were in a good spirit (especially when young members such as Half were on the receiving end); and resolving disagreements. It would be impossible to argue that continuing membership in the group was something not freely chosen by the core members for that two-year period.

Pave Jusup (aged 22 at date of interview), a leader and founding member of the MCF firm at Melbourne Knights, states consistent with the "loose ties" theory that the only things MCF members have in common are: (a) attending the games; (b) drugs and alcohol; and (c) Croatian heritage.16 However, he also suggests that the MCF is more organized than the firm at fellow Melbourne-based Croatian club, St Alban's (at date of interview it was a Victorian Premier League (VPL) club), in that the MCF is organized sufficiently to arrange bus trips interstate. In Pave's words: "[t]he supporters of St Alban's are not like us but they [also] do silly stuff. They are not organized like us. We are a proper group. They are just people that turn up at games and sing and drink a lot. We organize time at the pub and away trips". Our West Perth cheer squad lacked the ethnic heritage in common that the MCF has and drugs and alcohol were not part of the cheer squad's routine. However, at least after the first four or five weeks, the cheer squad was definitely, in Pave's words, a "proper group" just like the MCF is today. The group was a "group-for-itself" not just a "group-in-itself". The theoretical distinction between "group-for-itself" and "group-in-itself" appears to characterize the difference between the MCF and the St Alban's support.

The next character I will introduce to readers is the senior "Thommo", always known to the group members by the nickname of "Thommo" which he brought into the group from his home-suburb and high-school. Group members did coin some nicknames within the group. "Half" was the best and most famous of these. However, most of the nicknames people naturally brought into the group from outside and it were more authentic and simpler to use these pre-existing names than to invent new ones. Those nicknames brought in from outside the group and from outside West Perth football included "P.A." and "Thommo".

Mark "Thommo" Thompson's character was complex. He was, like many of the others, a working-class rebel and a very loyal and tough person. He could chat calmly and intelligently with people, but, if he felt that he was being disrespected, then he would change in an instant, and give that person a swift rebuke and stinging defence of himself and of his arguments. In that way people learned to respect him and be slightly wary of his reactions although you could also praise and respect him for his mild-mannered nature, self-control, and good humour. He was great for joking and laughter and he also enjoyed getting analytical at times about West Perth's players and performances.

Another point to note is that Thommo knew Courtney through junior football although they were not from the same high-school. Thommo then became an important natural link between the various sub-gangs in the group. His background, dressing, and style were more proletarian than those of the "Carine group", Courtney and Rohan. However, the link between Thommo and "the Carine group" was important and a part of the glue that reinforced trust and goodwill especially in those early weeks in 1984 when group members did not know each other well.

Cheer squad members all used to stay behind after games until well after darkness on the playing surface of Leederville Oval and the away venues to kick footballs amongst themselves. Thommo, in these encounters, was a fast, courageous, and skilful footballer. He would contest marks against the immobile rock that was P.A. who was six-feet-two and a veritable 18-year-old man mountain. P.A. would stand in one place to mark and kick whilst Thommo and the others would use their speed and skill to steal the marks from P.A., either in front or to the side of him, or else they would pick up the loose balls that P.A. spilled.

I can remember Thommo's habitual long-sleeved checked flannel shirts, later made famous in the grunge music era of the early-1990s, and how he would always have a cigarette packet in his chest pocket which would often fall to the ground whilst he was running at or with the football. He would then quickly run back to recover his cigarette packet from the ground in order to beat any potential "thieves". Group members stuck with their own group in these football games, and would never formally join in with strangers. This is perhaps further evidence for the proposition that the West Perth Cheer Squad was a "group-for-itself". It was an important relaxation and bonding time for the group members. It is unfortunate that AFL games do not allow the after-match kick on the field of play and this is another reason why attending WAFL or SANFL or the current VFL (formerly Victorian Football Association or VFA) games, at that second-tier level, can be a much more rewarding and enjoyable experience than attending AFL matches. Hunt and Bond write that: "Progress [in the AFL] has come at a cost, however, and one of the sacrifices the game has made is the kick-to-kick sessions on the ground after a match that we grew up with. And that's a shame".

My personal 1984 WAFL season notes, compiled during the 1984 season, state that Peter "P.A." Brennan (family name changed) (hereafter "P.A.") and Rex Tong (name changed) first joined the group for the Round 12 (23 June) 1984 match when West Perth defeated Claremont 21.10 (136) to 9.14 (68) at Subiaco Oval. Although at that time P.A. and R.T. were regarded by group members as being the "Balga group" R.T. was actually from Tuart Hill as he confirmed via a since self-deleted comment he posted on the WAFL Golden Era website (waflgoldenera.blogspot.com) on 14 June 2013. P.A. and R.T. together made an interesting spectacle, and I do remember that it was with great interest and some anxiety that group members watched the pair walk towards them on the first day. P.A. was six-feet-two, stocky, and built like a country league football ruckman (or like ruckman Ron Boucher of the Swan Districts Football Club) whereas R.T. was much shorter and quite slim. Together they could look quite comical.

Like Thommo, P.A. would aggressively defend himself (verbally) against anyone showing him disrespect. He would not use violence but instead he used scattered insults, teasing, and self-defensive analysis. He enjoyed the more extreme and crude banter and especially the cheer squad's insulting chants directed at the umpires and opposition players. He came from the working-class, government-housing estate of Balga, like the young West Perth player of that era and future North Melbourne AFL champion and coach, Dean Laidley (who played 70 games for West Perth, 1984-89 and 1991-92).

P.A. was totally loyal to the cheer squad and group members did their best to understand his strengths and weaknesses and to "accommodate" him. At times P.A. could surprise by his deeply analytical and calm discussions of football tactics and strategies; usually he would direct these statements to me as he presumed that I was either the group leader and / or the resident intellectual. At other times P.A. could be very childish. Mike B. was often annoyed by this childishness and he would threaten to leave the cheer squad and join the Grandstand Falcons but this never happened. Therefore, P.A. had his childish side and he also had his analytical side and people accepted these two sides of him.

P.A. had a subconscious tactic where, if he was being teased excessively, he would sometimes respond by quasi-analytical comments addressed to me (if I was not the main person doing the teasing). He would also get red in the face and break out in a silly grin when being teased which made him very vulnerable on the teasing front. He would bend down lower in his seated position as if to make a smaller target which was ridiculous given his height and bulky frame. P.A. was the oldest member of the group. I think his friend R.T. was two years younger than him or 16-years-old when the cheer squad first formed in 1984.

Rex Tong, the cheer squad's only Asian member, was an ethnic Chinese who also, from day one, wore the Bogan "uniform" of long-sleeved West Perth replica playing jersey and plain blue or black jeans (the most popular dressing style in the cheer squad). He was first seen with P.A. before they joined the group, and he also was associated with the "Balga group" although he came from Tuart Hill. He was also a very strange character and he had a love-hate relationship with P.A. that involved frequent insults directed at P.A.'s alleged stupidity and gullibility. It could be said that R.T. had a love-hate relationship with every group member. He spoke very good English, with a somewhat upper-class accent. R.T. was sarcastic and prickly, and he was extremely quick to defend himself. Group members felt that he must have encountered some severe racism which had led to the formation of his present personality. R.T. was on occasion verbally aggressive, sarcastic, insulting, and not highly liked. However, he was also loyal to the cheer squad for two years and I think that the people in the core group respected that fact. R.T. also enjoyed the intellectual discussions group members had about football tactics although he did not usually respect P.A.'s contributions. Early on he explained to the group that Peter B.'s nickname of "P.A." could be understood to mean either "Public Address System", because his voice was deep and loud, or be his initials as in "Peter Something". This second explanation made little sense as P.A.'s real name was allegedly Peter Brennan (family name changed) and his initials were P.B. However, group members accepted the explanations at face value because the nickname was clearly authentic and stranger things have happened out on the housing estates.

R.T. and P.A. often sat together and P.A. was usually in the group members' front row of seats directly behind the fence. I remember that he was often in the group's front row of people and so he (P.A.) would sometimes literally have to turn around to give me his analytical insights into the game in progress. An interesting coincidence was that West Perth's then league-team captain and one of the club's greatest ever players was Les Fong, a Chinese-Australian who was nicknamed "Chopsticks", "Choppy" or "Chopper", and then the cheer squad had its own Chinese member in R.T. Perhaps Les Fong's presence at West Perth made it easier for the cheer squad members to accept R.T. Their actual names in fact rhymed and had only two different letters out of seven. Group members regarded it as interesting, symmetrical, and appropriate that the cheer squad had its own Chinese member. It meant that the West Perth senior team squad had its mirror image, in terms of ethnic mix, on the other side of the playing fence.

I cannot remember R.T. facing any racism that was hostile from any of the cheer squad's core members but of course he may have experienced some teasing and put-downs. As with Thommo, R.T. had a very well-developed self-defence mechanism so people knew where they could stray verbally and where they could not. R.T. must have enjoyed cheer squad membership or he would not have stayed with us for two years. He was also a very faithful member even though he could never have been described as warm or even as friendly much of the time. He could also vary significantly in temperament and mood from week to week so on some weeks he might greet you warmly while on other weeks he might ignore a greeting. People had to work hard to earn his respect although he probably respected all or most of the cheer squad members, to some certain basic extent, if his continued attendance at games with the cheer squad was any indication. Of course people learned to expect D.S's mood changes and to live with them. I seem to recall that R.T. got on better with Courtney than with either Mike C. or Pete C. who were perhaps too "lumpenproletarian" for him.

One of R.T.'s strong points, other than his loyalty to the cheer squad, was that he would often laugh at the humour being shared around, and his face would sometimes light up in a wide and magnificent smile. If R.T. wanted to discuss something serious, he would come up very close to you, remove his black sunglasses, and quietly and carefully make his points. The removal of the "sunnies" was the sign of his respect and the seriousness of his point. R.T. loved the actual sport of Australian Rules more than most fans; watched each game pan out with eagle eyes (or perhaps we should say "with falcon eyes"); and he would rebuke people who made what he considered to be unnecessary noise. Sometimes the joking would set off among five or six group members. P.A. would double up, bend down lower, and emit loud laughs. R.T. would rarely laugh but he would have this wide smile while his eyes remained intently focused on the game! These were some of the better moments of the cheer squad. Despite this, I tended to keep R.T. at a distance, as did most people. However, R.T. clearly had a strong bond with P.A. that appeared to pre-date the day on which P.A and R.T. joined the cheer squad. The way the cheer squad worked was to honour and respect, and to some extent even to trust, these pre-existing bonds that people brought into the group from their home-suburbs and high-schools.

As mentioned, Mike C. and Pete C. were an integral part of the cheer squad from very early on. Cheer squad members knew that both had a background of reform homes, but no-one ever thought that either would steal anything from the group members or anything similar. Mike C. could find it hard to control his emotions, whether anger or excitement, so group members assumed his troubles with the police had related in some way to this. No-one ever asked him what his troubles had been. Pete C. once said that Mike "hated pigs" and no-one found this especially hard to believe. Cheer squad members adopted the "don't ask, don't tell" policy.

Mike C. was a scary sight to people that didn't know him and even to some of those who did. When he got excited by the football he would walk straight up to someone in the group, stand right in front of him, and totally invade his personal space, without seemingly being aware of it. He would also do this when greeting someone for the first time each match-day. His big green eyes got fiery when excited and, in his muscle tee-shirts of the 1980s and his long, thick, black, wavy hair, he cut a scary figure, and he was a vital part of the group's tough-guy image. Under his replica West Perth playing jersey, Mike C. would wear short-sleeved muscle tee-shirts, in bright colours, made famous by Australian rock stars of the era such as Cold Chisel's Jimmy Barnes and AC/DC's Bon Scott and Malcolm Young (6 January 1953 – 18 November 2017). Mike C. was at his most boisterous on West Perth's good days when he would loudly and gleefully start and continue chants and songs. Mike C. was completely unafraid of opposing supporters, enjoyed loudly and conspicuously "invading" opposing team's grounds, especially at Bassendean Oval, and he could become oblivious to place and context. Only the eight-year-old "Half" was as openly boisterous as Mike C. When excited, both individuals would cover large amounts of space in and near the cheer squad's chosen area, standing on and leaping over seats and waving flags and chanting.

Pete C. was a complete contrast to Mike C.: short, quiet, softly spoken, polite, thoughtful, gentle, analytical yet equally loyal – to his brother, to the cheer squad, and to the WPFC. He was one of the people whom I most enjoyed talking to. As with his brother Mike C., his standard match-day Bogan attire was long-sleeved West Perth replica jersey, tight blue or black jeans, and cheap sneakers. Both the brothers were fiercely loyal to each other and, of course, this fact and the underlying attitude behind it were very helpful to the cheer squad. Group members all valued the brothers' loyalty, warmth, and dedication to each other, to the group, and to West Perth. The C. brothers, along with Thommo and Robbie, gave the group much of its "illusion of violence" and the hooligan look and attitude. Group members knew that the C. brothers had no fixed abode and lived hand-to-mouth, and the group members thrived on this knowledge; it gave the cheer squad a working-class tough-guy persona that it might otherwise have lacked.

I now move on to mention the group's most important and
famous younger member, Michael, or "Half" as the group members
christened him because he was one-half the height of the other
people in the group. Half was a sandy-haired eight-year-old
whose parents were financial members of the West Perth Football
Club. They sat in the grandstand at home games and attended all
away games. They allowed Half to set his own agenda, go his own
way, and make his own friends during the games as long as he did
not leave the enclosed confines of the grounds. That was an era
where people generally let their children roam free and people
were less conscious of the threat of paedophiles. His parents
were never seen by the group members but I suppose that group
members viewed them as spectral support from the more
respectable section of the West Perth supporter base. They
attended all games home and away. Certainly they gave the group
a certain amount of trust and group members did feel some
obligation and responsibility regarding Half's welfare. Half was
a very passionate West Perth supporter although I believe he
lived in the East Perth FC geographic district in either
Bayswater or Maylands.

Half joined the cheer squad for every home and away game for
two years and he always joined group members on the playing
surface after games for the informal kick-to-kick sessions among
the group members. He was always regarded as an important part
of the cheer squad and his nickname was a sign of affection. He
was a carefree extrovert who liked chatting and laughing and
would get very excited during significant moments of play when
West Perth was doing well. At such times he would run around and
climb up on to empty seats, waving his flag furiously. He would
enjoy the insulting cheer squad chants and enjoy negative
discussions about other teams and verbally jousting with rival
fans of his own age if any of them came too close. Like every
group member, he genuinely loved and admired the playing group,
the team, and the club but in the innocent way you would expect
of an eight-year-old. When he urinated on the oval during kick-
to-kick sessions he would receive a rebuke from other members
who would quickly look away!

In 2011 Mike B. reminded me of an incident involving Half
which had not risen to the top of my memory and so had not made
the first draft of this book. At one particular game at
Leederville Oval, one of the teams was on a scoring spree and
the football would repeatedly sail over the wire fencing which
was and is only around eight metres behind the boundary fence at
the Technical School (northern) end of the ground. Half knew the
quickest way from the oval into the Technical School grounds
and, due to his knowledge of this route combined with his pace
and alertness, he was always first through to the Technical

School to recover the footballs. As Mike recounts the story, Half used to put the footballs under his jumper, re-enter the ground, and then give the footballs to his mother seated in the grandstand who was complicit in the thefts. One can only imagine the height and width of his perpetual cheeky grins on this particular afternoon! Mike says this occurred at many of the games but at one game in particular there was a scoring spree at the Technical School end and Half stole many footballs on this day alone. In the redevelopment of the ground over the past ten years the seats behind the goals and on the scoreboard wing have all gone but those in front of the tin shed, in the north-western corner of the ground, still remain today as they were in 1984.

Once I recall telephoning Half's house to discuss with him tickets relating to either the Sandover Medal Night, at the now demolished Perth Entertainment Centre in 1984, or to the first semi-final of 1985. I recall Half's father answering the phone and being very wary initially. However, when he heard that I was from "West Perth Cheer Squad", he totally relaxed, and he handed the phone over to Half. I arranged with Half for the buying of his ticket in conjunction with his father. Half could be quite mature in discussing things such as buying tickets to events. He certainly did not want to miss out on anything. Overall Half was an extremely interesting character and almost the cute and cheeky mascot of the cheer squad.

After the cheer squad membership had settled, Mike B. and I took the step as group founders to allow people to take home flags and banners after games on the proviso that the person bring the flag or banner to the game on the following Saturday. So although each flag still belonged to me, group members regarded the flags as "property in common". People felt pride in taking these flags back home and, in the case of most of the group members, back in the train and through the city-centre. Half and 13-year-old Tony travelled to the games in cars with their parents but I believe that both of them felt honoured to take flags back home and to be entrusted with this responsibility. I am not aware of any of the flags having gone missing during the two years. When the group effectively disbanded, early in the 1986 home-and-away season, I made no effort to claim back any of the flags and, to this day, I do not know where they are. I have never seen them resurface at games.

Sometime during the 1984 season, one group member made the surprising discovery that the red and blue floggers belonging to Fat Pam's cheer squad were still locked up in the storerooms of the club at Leederville Oval. "Floggers" are pieces, around 1.5 metres long; of coloured paper mache cut into strips around one inch or 2.5 cm wide and attached to a pole to be placed over the fence on match days and heaved up and down at significant moments. They look best in conjunction with flags which are waved higher up and behind them. Critchley cites Richmond's cheer squad leader, Gerard Egan, who says that Richmond switched over from paper mache to plastic floggers around 1985 or 1986 because the plastic floggers were not harmed in the rain. Critchley even offers a formal definition of "floggers"; clearly the name had been transplanted from Victorian cheer squad culture to Western Australia by 1984. Our group had only the old-style paper mache floggers but they were spared significant damage because, as mentioned, there were many fine-weather Saturdays during the 1984 season.

The cheer squad members took all of the Fat Pam group's floggers out, added them to the group's inventory of common property, and used them at each home game. The group members decided to deposit them in the club storerooms at Leederville Oval after home matches and use them only at the home games. The floggers were too cumbersome and bulky to take to away games and not quite "macho" enough to be seen with on trains or in the city-centre. I do not think that any floggers were lost or damaged during those two years as their numbers always seemed to be about the same week after week.

Group members routinely broke what is now an AFL rule for cheer squads and that was already a WAFL rule in 1984-85 but not regularly enforced. Group members positioned the floggers over, rather than behind, the boundary fence while not in use thus covering up the precious advertising signs. When the rule about these signs not being covered is enforced this represents movement to a higher stage of capitalism within the football industry since it allows businesses to place their interests above those of supporters even in absentia; thus the businesses can rule over supporters on match days even from beyond the physical confines of the stadium. Group members would argue with and insult any WAFL official who suggested that the group members should position the floggers inside the fence when not in use. To follow this regulation would have been silly as, firstly, the visual look from far off was important and, secondly, the floggers could be torn apart by people's shoes if positioned behind the fence. In the end no league or club official ever seriously challenged the group's collective moral authority with regards to the floggers' issue. Those were more innocent times when the hyper-capitalist elements in football were still emerging out of a more traditional and community-based football culture and the hyper-capitalist and politically-correct elements were not yet then clearly dominant (as is the case at AFL level today).

Then, as mentioned previously, there were the two overweight Italian brothers, the elder Tony aged 13 and the younger Mario aged around 9. Tony had a friend, Ben McA (pictured below), who was around 13-14-years-old and a head or so taller than Tony. Years later I became a Facebook friend of the same Ben McA. The three would always sit together and always wear the West Perth long-sleeved replica playing jerseys. Tony may have attended Perth Modern Senior High School as did his friend Rob, who was also a cheer squad member. Rob was also a friend of Ben but Ben attended the Catholic college John XXIII.17 Cheer squad members often saw the father of Tony and Mario with his younger boys and girls, dropping the brothers off or watching the group quietly at a distance.

Ben, Rob, and Tony were very shy and quiet people. They were eager to please; they respected the group as a group-for-itself probably more than anyone else did; and they attended all or most of the home-and-away games. Tony, in particular, regarded it as an honour and a responsibility to be allowed to take flags home with him each week. Mike B. and I knew that at least he would not lose any on the train (he travelled by car) and so we entrusted him with more than one flag. Ben, Rob, and Tony were, as mentioned, shy lads who enjoyed the group but they tried much of the time to avoid upsetting people or outstaying their presumed welcome.

I recall that Tony and Mario were there, wearing as was their custom their long-sleeved West Perth replica jerseys, when the cheer squad attended Channel Seven's "World of Football" programme shot live on a Sunday from the social club rooms at Leederville Oval. The cheer squad also attended when the programme was shot live on another Sunday from Bassendean Oval social club rooms, home of Swan Districts Football Club. Non-club members were welcome to these events, and they helped to bring the game and the media closer to the grassroots supporters, and broke down the divide between paid-up club members and ordinary supporters. With these events alienation between football supporters was broken down and a more communal spirit began to operate. These events were typical of a more innocent era, although, paradoxically, behind the scenes at this time an independent WAFL Commission had been set up to replace traditional leadership by the eight clubs. Furthermore, within a year or two this Commission, led by St George's Terrace businesspersons such as John Walker, Richard Colless, and Peter Fogarty, would pay the exorbitant fee of AUD4 million to join an expanded VFL competition through new super-team West Coast Eagles formed as part of the soon-to-fail sports and entertainment listed corporation Indian Pacific Limited (IPL). It was really true that, dialectically, everything morphs into its opposite, as Mao Zedong wrote, or "it's always darkest before the dawn". Just as the powerbrokers of the WAFL and the media were taking the game back to the grassroots, by the "World of Football" live shoots and the open public invitation to the 1984 Sandover Medal Night, rising corporatism, of a particularly arrogant and unpleasant kind, was about to change the game irrevocably in Western Australia. When the vote of WAFL club presidents was held on 22 August 1986 to see whether the state would join the expanded VFL for 1987, only Bill Walker of Swan Districts and South Fremantle's Wayne Ryder, to their eternal credit, voted "no".

I related well to Ben, Rob, and Tony and I think that they were closer to Mike B. and me than to any of the others. Without meaning to sound disrespectful towards them, they were the nearest the group had to anonymous "foot-soldiers" whereas all the others were brash and extroverted personalities, except perhaps for Pete C. and Rohan. Ben, Rob, and Tony respected the cheer squad as an organized group or a group-for-itself. They were old enough to know what the cheer squad was all about but young enough to regard the group from a certain objective distance because they were slightly too young to relate on equal terms with the core members.

Ben, Rob, and Tony gave the group some existential and moral legitimacy as being something more than just a group of mates. They regarded the cheer squad as a legitimate organization and Mike B. and I felt honoured because of that trust and respect. We felt some sort of an obligation to look after them and to include them in all group activities. Because they were happy to be foot-soldiers, the trio was not teased overly much and cheer squad members appreciated their presence whereas if the group had been just a group of mates the group members might have tried to shake them off. The cheer squad was a "public" group, to use today's Facebook terminology, and open to all. Again the ethnic composition of the group mirrored that of West Perth's playing group: West Perth's league-team of this era had Chinese-Australian rover Les Fong and Italian-Australian ruck-rover Peter Menaglio (236 games played, 1977-89), and the cheer squad also had its Chinese and Italian members. As mentioned, cheer squad members felt that there was something symmetrical and appropriate about this.

I shall next mention "Robbie" who was the only full-time core member, if my memory serves me correctly, who joined the cheer squad for the 1985 season having not been a member in 1984. Robbie was a friend of Thommo's from junior football and he also knew P.A. because of the Balga connection. Therefore, like Thommo, he was a natural link between sub-gangs and part of the glue between sub-gangs that held the broader cheer squad

together. Blond-haired Robbie considered himself something of a
star footballer and I recall that an actual football never left
his hands. It was a big yellow one and he was always bouncing it
on the ground and handballing it to himself.

Robbie was easily distracted and always talking to someone.
Often he would sit on the first or second row and turn around to
face the rear so that he could continually talk to people. I did
not regard highly him doing this as he was not watching the game
and I could probably be authoritarian at times with the looks
that I gave! According to cheer squad ethics and etiquette, the
reserves game, the half-time break, and after-the-game are the
times reserved for socializing whereas people should watch the
main game intently. If you are not watching the game how can you
know when to wave the flags? Cheer squads are not like Sydney
United's Edensor Park Ultras, in New South Wales Premier League
(NSWPL) soccer, who chant and bang drums throughout the match,
on a continuous basis, and hence do not really have to watch the
game. Unlike soccer ultras, a cheer squad does not chant and
sing continually. I felt that there was plenty of time for
everybody to claim their coveted seats behind the goals and to
socialize before the start of the main game which, in those
days, was always at 2.20pm. The after-match ritual is discussed
in the next chapter.

I could not relate very well to Robbie but that probably
reflected my problems and limitations as much as or more than it
reflected Robbie's. Robbie had a characteristic of not looking a
person in the eyes during a conversation. I tended to avoid
talking to him, but I realized that the cheer squad needed all
the committed core members that it could find. I was pleased
that Robbie did have a number of people that he could relate to
well within the group and his connection with Thommo was very
strong. Robbie was also one of those people who very much
enjoyed teasing P.A. If I am not mistaken I think that Robbie
also lived in Balga but I would not put Robbie unambiguously in
the "Balga faction". Instead Robbie was a "floater" who operated
between sub-gangs and was closer to Thommo who also never really
had a sub-gang (see Appendix A).

Lastly, I should mention the brother or step-brother of Mike
C. and Pete C., Robert C. He was understood to be a more
hardcore juvenile delinquent than either Mike or Pete. Cheer
squad members knew of or heard about the offence he had
allegedly served time for and it was quite a serious offence
although I will not name it here. Robert (never "Rob" or
"Robbie") joined the cheer squad on two or three occasions and
group members made him feel welcome and he enjoyed the group. In
terms of Robert's personality, he could be placed halfway
between the extroverted Mike C. and the introverted Pete C.

Robert was also in between the ages of Pete and Mike so around
15-years-old in 1984. Robert was fairly quiet when he was with
the cheer squad but possibly that was because he did not know
most of the group members well. Like all the others, he
respected people and he gave no-one any trouble. Finally, Mike
and Pete C. had a four-year-old girl niece (or cousin) whom they
would sometimes supervise and drag around at matches. She
probably came to games about as often as she did not.

In terms of the social class of the cheer squad, how does it
compare to Eric Dunning's "rougher sections of the working-
class", Gary Armstrong et al.'s "working-class in general" and /
or John Hughson's "upper-level or respectable part of the
working-class in comfortable homes"? We could use two criteria:
suburb where the person lived and / or more subjective factors
such as personal style, manner of speaking, and dressing style.
I will not go beyond the first criteria here. The group had a
Carine group of two and a Booragoon group of two which can both
be placed in the middle-class or professional middle-class. The
group had a "Balga faction" of two and two others connected to
that suburb and the group had the C. brothers who had spent
considerable time in reform homes and were commonly perceived as
having no fixed abode.

Balga has traditionally been perceived to be semi-criminal
government housing. Wikipedia states that "[t]he name 'Balga'
was adopted in 1954 and is the Noongar (Australian Aboriginal)
word for the indigenous grass tree Xanthorrhoea preissii". I can
recall, around 1996 or 1997, my car running out of petrol on
Wanneroo Road in Balga on my way back home to Merriwa. Night was
coming and I had to walk with my empty petrol can through the
suburb to a service station. One man joined me on my walk, as he
was heading in the same direction. The man was cheerful and
friendly enough but he did show me a knife kept down under the
lower leg of his jeans. That incident would be consistent with
many outsiders' perceptions of a typical Balga day. Wikipedia
writes further about Balga as follows:

"At the 2006 census, Balga had a population of 8,494.
Balga residents had a median age of 34, and median incomes were
well below average for the Perth metropolitan area and the
region — $347 per week compared with $513 per week in Perth, and
$526 in the North Metropolitan statistical region. The
population of Balga was more ethnically diverse than the Perth
average, with 57.7% born in Australia and significant minorities
from Sudan, Italy, Macedonia, Vietnam and Burma identified in
the 2006 census. At the 2006 census, 4.49% of residents
identified as Indigenous Australians".

The more "respectable" southern half of the suburb managed to later (1994) get a name change to Westminster which downgraded the remaining Balga section still further in some people's eyes. The move to get the Westminster name (with its English-Establishment as opposed to Australian Aboriginal origins) shows the social stigma attached to the Balga name by certain people. However, clearly Balga's residents in 1984 and 1985 would have included fully-employed working-class and unemployed or underemployed "lumpenproletariat" or "dangerous classes". It would then have resembled the Whitechapel and Spitalfields of the era of the "Jack the Ripper" murders in 1888 East London where social historians indicate that respectable members of the working-class and some professional people lived on the main thoroughfares such as Commercial Road, Commercial Street, and Whitechapel High Street. By contrast, the rougher and semi-criminal elements lived hand-to-mouth existences in "the evil quarter mile" which included the doss-houses of Dorset Street, Flower and Dean Street, Fashion Street, and Brick Lane.

Our group members were from mixed social backgrounds: the group had middle-class and lumpenproletarians (to use the traditional Marxist term) all lumped in together but the group members made it operate successfully for two years.

There was an egalitarian and fraternal atmosphere between the cheer squad members and the equivalent groups from other clubs consistent with the culture and the ethics of the Victorian and South Australian cheer squads of the era. As an example of Victorian cheer squad ethics in the 1970s and 1980s, members from different cheer squads used to shout the final match scores from their respective grounds across railway station platforms at Melbourne's Flinders Street station on Saturday evenings. There was also a place called Classic Cafe in Melbourne city-centre where cheer squad members from different clubs would congregate and interact on Saturday nights after the regular home-and-away games. In terms of WAFL cheer squad ethics, the cheer squad leaders' relationships with Perth and Claremont cheer squad members at grounds and in the city-centre were always cordial. Perth's cheer squad leader, Nick, and the Claremont cheer squad leader(s) might have been expatriate Victorians since they operated their respective cheer squads in the Victorian manner.

There was a combined Perth-Claremont cheer squad which unofficially represented Western Australia in the state match against Victoria at Subiaco Oval on Tuesday afternoon 17 July 1984.18 The Perth-Claremont group invited the West Perth Cheer Squad to join them but the West Perth group declined so that people in this group could attend separately with their own various gangs of school mates. The match was held on a school day (Tuesday) afternoon and so people "wagged" (skipped) school or work to go to the game. Being on a school day it made logistic sense to attend this match with school-mates rather than with "Saturday's heroes" because planning for the day could take place at school on the Monday. Also Mike B. and I felt that the ethical requirement to attend with school-mates overrode the ethical requirement to attend with the cheer squad since the match took place during school hours on a school day.

I now move on to discuss key opponents and big matches involving those teams. First we should mention Claremont. Traditionally Claremont has been regarded as the club of and for the "college boys" and the club has long been associated with an amateur approach to the game. Although only one thousand people attended the match, the difference in culture and attitudes of the Claremont versus Port Adelaide Magpies supporters at the Subiaco Oval Foxtel Cup clash on 16 July 2011 was quite apparent. To cite the Full Points Footy website about Claremont supporters:

"For much of its history, if Dave Warner is to be believed, 'Claremont's supporters would arrive at the outer of other clubs, erect their deckchairs and then complain when other fans stood in front'. Prior to the 1980s Claremont were cream-puff, card-carrying nancy [sic] boys, but that has all changed and nowadays Claremont are rarely seen down the puce [sic] end of town".

To be fair, Full Points Footy does point out that: "Premiership pennants in elite Australian football competitions ... quite simply do not end up in the possession of ineffectual weaklings, and Claremont produced a number of flag-winning combinations well before the 1980s". However, despite this, Claremont fans generally were not feared. No-one went to Claremont Oval the least bit apprehensive about the home-team supporters.

By the late-1970s and early-1980s, the club had shaken off its college boy image and pieced together, under the coaching of first Mal Brown and then Essendon Brownlow Medallist Graham Moss, a formidable collection of talented footballers, many of whom would go on to play VFL/AFL football. These talented footballers included Mike "Doc" Aitken (Carlton); John Annear (Collingwood, Richmond, and West Coast); Wayne Blackwell (Carlton); Allen "Shorty" Daniels (Footscray); Ken Hunter (Carlton); Jim and Phil Krakouer (North Melbourne, St Kilda, and Footscray); and Warren Ralph (Carlton). As the Full Points Footy website comments: "Moss coached Claremont for ten seasons, during which time the club fielded some of the most star-studded line ups in Western Australian football history". In the 1981 grand-final, Claremont was formidable, using the powerful combination of Graham Moss (ruck), Jim Krakouer (rover), and Warren Ralph (full-forward), to defeat a very strong South Fremantle team. Curtin University's Sean Gorman, in his book on Jim and Phil Krakouer, provides a detailed description of this violent match. In the late-1980s, the Claremont club would go on to produce the outstanding West Coast players Chris Lewis and Guy McKenna.

Unfortunately, for the brilliant Claremont, the club was not the only WAFL powerhouse of the early-1980s. In terms of not only individual playing talent but also well-drilled, well-disciplined, and well-coached teams, the WAFL of the early- to mid-1980s was remarkable. In most eras Moss's Claremont would have won more than the one premiership but it simply could not defeat the brilliant, emergent Swan Districts with Swans defeating Claremont in both the 1982 and 1983 grand-finals. The Claremont club historian Kevin Casey writes that many long-term Claremont supporters believe that the Tigers should have won three premierships during the coaching reign of Graham Moss (1977-86). Similarly, John Todd made the comparison with the West Perth team of the early-1950s which was excellent but always just one step below the South Fremantle team of that era. Dawson writes that: "The greater versatility of the Swans sides, plus an edge in mental toughness, were important factors in denying Claremont premiership success in 1982 and '83, according to John [Todd], who felt the Tigers probably had an edge in talent".

I can clearly remember trying to place a bet with the Claremont supporter and mathematics teacher at Applecross Senior High School, Mrs. Machin, on the 1982 or 1983 grand-final result, only to be told (and this is definitely an exact quote): "I don't bet with students"! She was quite wise since, regardless of the year, my money would have been on Swans and I would have won. By 1984 and 1985 the Claremont star had begun to fade as the player drain to the VFL/AFL had taken most of the talent out of the team. By 1984-85, Ron Alexander's East Fremantle and Haydn Bunton Junior's Subiaco were the emerging power teams as Swan Districts and Claremont had been five years earlier. Both these clubs, East Fremantle and Subiaco, contested the last two grand-finals of the pre-West Coast era, with East Fremantle winning narrowly in 1985 and Subiaco winning convincingly in 1986.

The West Perth Cheer Squad had a good relationship with Claremont's cheer squad which congregated behind the northern-end goals at Claremont Oval. Their leader was a friendly, tall, brown-haired guy who had a Victorian style duffel coat with "Claremont Peter 15 Jamieson" on the back. I either can't recall

or never knew his name. Our cheer squad took a large group to
Claremont Oval once or twice in 1984 and 1985. I can only
remember single trips to Bassendean Oval, Claremont Oval,
Lathlain Park, Subiaco Oval, and Perth Oval, but the records
suggest more than one game at those venues from May 1984 to
August 1985. Therefore, either the cheer squad only attended
once or my memory has conflated two visits into one for some or
all of those venues.

Claremont's cheer squad was enthusiastic and dedicated and
the West Perth Cheer Squad certainly respected it. At Claremont
Oval, the West Perth Cheer Squad occupied the seats behind the
southern-end goals while the Claremont Cheer Squad sat behind
the northern-end goals. They had to pass by the West Perth Cheer
Squad to get to their seats since they mostly arrived from
Claremont train station at the oval's southern-end; whenever we
met our two groups exchanged friendly greetings. Claremont had
probably the second-largest and best-organized cheer squad
behind Perth FC in 1984 and 1985. I believe that both groups
were probably led by expatriate Victorians who operated the
cheer squads in line with Victorian cheer squad culture and
ethics. At Claremont Oval the West Perth Cheer Squad matched the
Claremont Cheer Squad in terms of the total number of flags and
banners although the West Perth group as usual (for away games)
did not bring its floggers. The West Perth cheer squad members
were especially proud of the group's 1.2 metre x 1.2 metre "Cop
That" banner.

At away games, especially, there was a carnival atmosphere
among our cheer squad because cheer squad members felt no
"obligation" or "responsibility" in terms of defending home-team
territory or honour. It was like a day-out or a day at the
seaside as most people did not normally travel to other parts of
the metropolitan area, being constrained by school commitments,
public transport timetables, and personal finances. When cheer
squad members saw people arrive during the reserves game, in
dribs and drabs of singles, twos, and threes, the newcomers
would each receive a warm welcome. Many people, especially in
the cheer squad's first year, would walk towards our group
hesitatingly and a warm welcome was needed to get them to sit
with our group. At away games it was impossible to know how many
people the cheer squad would get. Non-regulars would often
congregate with the cheer squad at away games as the cheer squad
was the most visible group of West Perth support. In addition to
the cheer squad there was always Grandstand Falcons in the
grandstand, a supporters' group which had no flags or banners
but was made up of hearty singers and chanters (refer back to
Chapter 1). That group's members were a few years older than the

cheer squad members (they were probably then in their twenties)
but the cheer squad members knew them all by sight.

In the early- and mid-1980s, West Perth had a reasonable
team and, even if it finished fifth or sixth at the end of the
season, on any given day you would give the team at least a 40%
chance of winning no matter whom the opposition was. As the Full
Points Footy website recounts, West Perth inherited from the
Graham Farmer years in the late-1960s and early-1970s a fast,
skilful, run-on style of play especially suited to the team's
speedy on-ballers such as Ron Davis (13 games played, 1984-85);
Les Fong; John Gastevich (61 games, 1983-88); Ross Gibbs (97
games, 1979-83); Derek Kickett (38 games, 1984-86); Dean
Laidley; Peter Menaglio (236 games, 1977-89); George Michalczyk
(58 games, 1982-86); Peter Murnane (36 games, 1982, 1985-87);
David Palm (91 games, 1980-82, 1990-91); and the late Chris
Stasinowsky (51 games, 1979-82). As the Full Points Footy
website explains, citing Farmer himself halfway through the
quote:

"Under Farmer, West Perth developed a fast, open, play on brand
of football similar in style to that produced by Geelong in the
VFL, or Sturt in South Australia. The club's training regime
maximised physical fitness, endeavoured to habituate players to
the sorts of psychological pressure and physical duress they
could anticipate during matches, and inculcated in them the
importance of making the best possible decision, from a range of
alternatives, whenever they gained possession of the ball. As
Farmer himself remarked, 'My basis of football was to develop a
natural habit, where people automatically responded in the
correct manner. The first commitment is always to get the ball;
it's what you do with the ball after that that will decide how
far you take it down the field. If there were five or six
variables to make a play, they had to pick the right one.......
The basis of my training was always to give it to a footballer
who was moving down the field. We were giving them the ball as
they were moving down the field'".

Furthermore, a leading football writer with The West Australian,
Gary Stocks described West Perth in 1986 as follows: "West Perth
are widely regarded as league football's most skilful team".
Strong ruckmen and physical players were the team's weaknesses.
Generally the key forward and back positions down the centre of
the ground, excluding centre-half-forward in the years when
either Brian Adamson or Phil Bradmore held down the position,
were the team's weak areas. Especially if a key player was
injured the team would often run into difficulties. Key position
defenders, Graeme Comerford (80 games, 1982-86) and 1975

premiership player Geoff Hendriks, were effective and dependable - albeit not as charismatic as former full-back, the earringed and mulleted Ray Holden (102 games, 1979-83, 1987-89), who departed for Melbourne (VFL/AFL) at the end of the 1983 season.

West Perth was fortunate in that, one year after Ben Jager (135 games, 1977-83), its first-choice lead ruckman since the late-1970s, retired, John Duckworth returned to the playing field. However, Duckworth mainly played centre-half-back in 1985 with new country recruit, 24-year-old Kim Rogers from Tammin (29 games, 1985-86), performing remarkably well in Jager's place. In fact Rogers' rise was a major explanatory factor behind West Perth's return to final round football in 1985. The return of the former Hawthorn premiership player Peter Murnane and the veteran rover Corry Bewick (128 games, 1977-82 and 1985-86) and the debut of Darren Bewick (52 games, 1985-87) were also significant events for the senior team and for the club in 1985. Murnane had given the team maturity, poise, drive, and class in the centre of the ground and he had proved hard to replace. He was definitely one reason why the team had excelled on-the-field in the 1982 season and then struggled in the subsequent two years. The ex-Hawthorn premiership player's VFL/AFL experience had made him more of a strategic thinker and he was mentally harder and less error-prone than many WAFL footballers.

West Perth did have a strong backline in the early- and mid-1980s, with the reliable Perth defender Neil Fotheringhame (64 games, 1980-83 and 66 games for Perth from 1975-79) crossing over to West Perth, while Ross Prunster (159 games, 1973-79 and 36 games for Perth in 1980-81 and 1984) and Mark Washfold (41 games, 1978-80 and 66 games for Perth from 1981-84) went the other way. Other players involved in this lively cross-town traffic between Perth and West Perth were Doug Simms to West Perth (32 games, 1983-85 and 93 games for Perth from 1977-83) and, in the opposite direction, John Gavranich (39 games, 1980-83 and 126 games for Perth from 1984-91), Mick Rea (21 games, 1979-81 and 121 games for Perth from 1981-88), and the late Chris Stasinowsky (51 games, 1979-82 and 31 games for Perth from 1985-86). Atkinson writes as follows: "Chris Stasinowsky also played 26 games for South Fremantle in 1982-1984. He kicked 11 goals against West Perth in one game".19 Without wanting to cast aspersions on the fine contributions made to West Perth by both Fotheringhame and Simms, it is far from certain, based on the information presented in this paragraph, that West Perth got the best out of its trades with Perth during the drought era. With so many trades between the two clubs, with hindsight, it is easily possible to perceive the two clubs as having been one. If a merger had to happen, a West Perth merger with Perth would be far more palatable to me than a merger with East Perth, the

traditional enemy of both Perth and West Perth. I am sure that
many Perth supporters would agree with these sentiments.

West Perth also received good service from its South
Fremantle recruits, wingman Phil Cronan (22 games, 1983) and
rover Paul Mountain (21 games, 1983), although, unfortunately,
neither remained at the club beyond the single season. It is
interesting to note that very few or no West Perth players
crossed from West Perth to East Perth during the pre-West Coast
era. This perhaps reveals the depth of negative feeling between
the two clubs. One of the few players to head in the opposite
direction, in the post-Polly Farmer years, was centre-man George
Michalczyk. Although not quite as much of a sensation as Maurice
"Mo" Johnston's 1989 move from Celtic to Rangers, where he
became that club's first high-profile Roman Catholic player,
Michalczyk's "defection" from East Perth was very well received
at its cross-town rival and he would later go on to coach West
Perth.

Generally West Perth struggled in wet weather and the team
also struggled against very strong physical teams although
occasionally such teams would be showed up by the Cardinals for
their lack of pace and sixth sense. Especially at Leederville
Oval, on beautiful fine winter days with the home crowd in full
voice, West Perth played brilliant football during the
premiership drought era (1976-86) and it was more than capable
of inflicting defeat upon any team. Statistically this is the
case as Atkinson's history section shows that, in the pre-West
Coast Eagles section of the drought era from 1976-86, West Perth
often defeated the eventual premier team twice in a season,
including Perth in 1977 (two wins); East Perth in 1978 (two
wins); Swan Districts in 1982 (two wins) and 1984 (two wins);
and East Fremantle in 1985 (two wins). This remains a strong
record but it is also a clear case of potential unfulfilled.
Although the club did not suffer the same exodus of players to
Victoria as other higher-profile and trendier teams, Ross Gibbs
later played 253 games (1984-94) for Glenelg in the SANFL,
including the two pre-Adelaide Crows era premierships of 1985-
86, and David Palm was a strong and consistent contributor at
Richmond in the VFL/AFL (104 games, 1983-88). Palm developed
into a consistent centre-man for Richmond over a number of years
and he deserves to be mentioned in the same breath as the
legendary Richmond centre-men who preceded him in that position
Geoff Raines and the late Maurice Rioli.

Perhaps West Perth's best known football exports, in the
post-Farmer era, have been Darren Bewick, Derek Kickett, and
Dean Laidley as well as the coach turned football commentator
Dennis Cometti. Generally West Perth's best players were
undervalued and under-recognized during the drought era.

Contemporaneous newspaper reports in The West Australian refer
to both Bradmore and Menaglio as "underrated" suggesting that
they should have polled more Sandover Medal votes than they did.
For example, Gary Stocks, in his 1985 first semi-final match
report, states that: "Bradmore received a meagre total of 14
[1985 Sandover] medal votes, a classic case of where the work
done by a player during a season was undervalued". In relation
to the 1985 first semi-final, Stocks went on to say that
Bradmore was "the best man afield ... in the opinion of some".
About the inaugural Eagles squad member, John Gastev (who was
originally known as John Gastevich), Stocks comments as follows
after the first West Perth game of the 1987 season versus East
Perth: "He is one of the most underrated players in WA, with the
ability to win the hard ball and pinpoint delivery".

SANDOVER MEDAL NIGHT
MONDAY 27.8.1984
I will now discuss the WAFL Sandover Medal Night held at the now
demolished Perth Entertainment Centre on Monday 27 August 1984.
This was the first time ever that the fairest-and-best player
award presentation night had been opened to the general public
and it has never been opened to the public again. I view the
move as part of an effort to "take the game to the people", a
move towards empowerment, at the same time as the WAFL
commissioners were simultaneously disempowering people by
negotiating to be part of an expanded VFL over the heads of the
ordinary club supporters and even over two club presidents.

The Perth Entertainment Centre (opened on 27 December 1974
and closed in August 2002) held around 8,200 people. Tickets
were sold to the Sandover Medal Count for a reasonable fee,
three dollars per person or around the cost of a match-day
concession ticket, and supporters were allocated specific areas
within the venue according to the club they supported. Our group
made an effort to attend and secure tickets for the members and
for the younger people in the group such as Half and Thommo
Junior (Thommo's younger brother aged around eight). Given that
the Medal Night was held on a weekday, winter's evening in a
city-centre venue (in an era prior to mass gentrification of the
inner-city) not surprisingly the main group of people in
attendance were the hardcore cheer squad members carrying their
big flags and banners. Perth, Claremont, Subiaco, West Perth,
and East Perth all had large vocal cheer squad groups at the
venue that night. Of course our group cheered and waved its
flags when a West Perth player received a vote just as we would
have done behind the goals on any match day. Fitting in with the
carnival mood of the whole evening, there were three tied

winners of the award, Michael Mitchell and Steve Malaxos of Claremont and Peter Spencer of East Perth.

The football historian Tony Barker is extremely unfair when he writes that: "The result was far more discordant then the mere presence of women could have been, with up to 3,000 fans jeering the tallying of votes for players from rival clubs". I was there and the general behaviour that night was very good because the crowd was made up in large part of young and dedicated football supporters most of whom were cheer squad members and under the supervision of cheer squad leaders. The back page of The West Australian on the Wednesday after the Monday night count was very critical of the event and the booing and jeering of flag-waving supporters. Various identities were trotted out to condemn the night. Surprisingly, it was not The West Australian's chief sporting writer, the late Geoff Christian (1934-98), who wrote the piece but some unknown female journalist, Linda Byrne, perhaps drafted in from the front section of the newspaper. One wonders even whether the reporting of the Monday night medal count was held back until the Wednesday paper so that the count results were not reported prior to the reporting of the public backlash.

The sensationalist article by Byrne opens as follows: "Telephone switchboards ran hot at West Australian Newspapers, Channel 7 and talk-back radio programmes yesterday as people protested about the handling of this year's Sandover Medal presentation". The writer goes on to explain how callers were "disgusted" because the "winners were booed by jeering flag-waving fans" during the two-hour event which was also telecast live by Channel 7. George Michalczyk of West Perth was forthright, hostile, and even a tad moralistic and superior in his comments spoken in his capacity as head of the Players' Association: "It was a commercial failure and a TV failure. I don't think there are any positive things to say for it. I think the general public reaction will say that this will never happen again at the Entertainment Centre". Of course the vast majority of the fans present enjoyed themselves tremendously by behaving exactly as they would on any match day. Michalczyk need not have worried himself too much: by 1987 most of these noisy, teenaged, flag-waving fans would stop attending WAFL games (having shifted over to support West Coast Eagles in the expanded VFL).

Somewhat more tactfully than most commentators and not wanting to upset either the moralizers or the fans, the then WAFL president Vince Yovich simply said that the event "lacked atmosphere" which it may have done, from the TV perspective, because of the cavernous and generic nature of the venue. To his credit, East Fremantle's coach Ron Alexander simply gave full marks to Channel 7 for attempting something different. A Channel

7 spokesperson, station manager Mr. Alan Richards, was misquoted
by Linda Byrne, perhaps deliberately. At the start of the back
page article Richards is proclaimed as having been surprised by
the hostile reaction and Byrne takes this to mean the hostile
reactions of the supporters on the night. In fact his full quote
appears later in the same article and it is very clear that he
is expressing surprise at the "hostile reactions" of the people
who contacted TV and radio stations and the newspaper to
complain about the count on the day after the event. Richards
correctly and sensibly pointed out that the fan reaction on that
night was the same as you would hear on the terraces on any
match-day. In Richards' words: "As a television person watching
the event last night I thought it was the right approach and was
somewhat surprised by the reaction". Clearly the reaction
Richards is referring to here is that of the bourgeois, public
policers of decency and decorum on the Tuesday rather than the
reaction of the fans at the count on the Monday night. You
cannot invite the public to a venue known for loud rock concerts
by bands such as AC/DC and KISS and charge a very cheap
admission price and then realistically expect black-tie, gala-
dinner behaviour.

The moralistic public uproar resulted in the 1985 medal
count night being shifted back to its traditional venue, The
Golden Ballroom of the Sheraton Perth Hotel, and the ordinary
supporters were again excluded. Nowadays the Brownlow (AFL) and
Sandover Medal (WAFL) nights are corporate events at luxury
hotel ballrooms, and players and WAGS (wives and girlfriends)
dress up in their showy fineries. The counts have become fashion
shows and places to be seen. Carlton AFL player Brendan Fevola's
behaviour at the 2009 Brownlow Medal Count included vomiting,
swearing, spilling beer, simulated sex acts, and molestation of
women. No teenage cheer squad member behaved in such ways at the
Perth Entertainment Centre in August 1984 although some of us
might have accidentally spilled our soft-drinks! Nonetheless,
the ruling-class of football decided that it most definitely did
not want the lumpenproletariat supporters to be in such close
proximity at future counts. There was even an early sneaky
attempt to erase the 1984 Sandover Medal Count Night from
football history with the 1985 edition of Christian et al.'s The
Footballers book mentioning neither the count night nor the
three winners' names (but including the three winners in the
list of medal winners on page 183).

East Perth Football Club was and still remains today West
Perth's arch-rivals. East Perth was a strong club throughout the
1960s and up to 1978. However, the Perth Oval-based club
generally failed to match it in the 1980s with the new
powerhouses South Fremantle, Claremont, and Swan Districts (in

the early-1980s) and East Fremantle and Subiaco (in the mid-1980s). The East Perth club had possibly begun to suffer the after-effects of a declining junior base in its inner-city areas, a factor that may also partially explain Perth FC's poor years from 1980 onwards. The declining junior base was the primary factor behind West Perth's 1994 move to a more lucrative junior zone in the Joondalup area in Perth's outer northern suburbs. In hindsight, perhaps, the 1978 grand-final between East Perth and Perth represented the end of an era, the last hurrah of the traditional inner-city clubs.

My belief then was that East Perth supporters were an overly serious and macho bunch that believed that their team was the toughest and most ruthless. They generally did not respect other clubs at all and especially West Perth. It was mostly East Perth fans who used the racist "Garlic Muncher" tag for West Perth supporters because, like South Fremantle, West Perth had always been (or at least since the 1950s) a multicultural club both in terms of its playing squads and its supporter base. The club welcomed these supporters and players and gained a reputation as a multicultural club. Both West Perth and South Fremantle represent districts with large Croatian / Yugoslav and Italian populations. Most of the ethnic soccer clubs, associated with the Croatian, Greek, and Italian communities, are based in the West Perth and South Fremantle catchment areas. Despite this, South Fremantle has never been burdened by a tag such as "Garlic Munchers" possibly because East Fremantle fans have always been far too gentlemanly and self-assured of their own worth to resort to such insulting labelling of a rival club. The other six WAFL clubs tended to be more strictly Anglo in the 1970s and 1980s, although East Perth and Swan Districts have had significant numbers of Aboriginal players and supporters.

The official "Royals" nickname for the East Perth club was an enigma. On the one hand, I felt that some East Perth supporters were somewhat embarrassed by it because it did not gel neatly with their working-class (Aussie not British) tough-guy image. This interpretation is based on the "Australia as a rugged colony" tradition which played a major role in Ashes Test cricket matches in the 1970s. On the other hand, the Royals' nickname for East Perth and the club's crown symbol could have been viewed in white-supremacist / British nationalist terms. If this meaning wasn't overt during the 1980s (it clearly wasn't) it was arguably at least there in the background playing with people's collective subconscious, and especially those of West Perth supporters when they were hit with the "Garlic Munchers" tag. It is unfortunate that political correctness arrived too late and Royals' fans were not castigated for their insulting use of the racist "Garlic Munchers" label for West Perth fans during the WAFL's Golden Era. In the 1980s East Perth and East Fremantle fans were probably those least likely to wear club colours at their games although this is admittedly a subjective memory.

Our West Perth Cheer Squad believed that East Perth players and fans took themselves too seriously and lacked charm and humour. The cheer squad members also felt that, although both clubs were mid-table in 1984-85, West Perth had a faster running and more skilful side. West Perth fans thought that West Perth's 1982 recruitment of East Perth centreman George Michalczyk (whose nephew is the West Coast Eagles player Dean Cox) was a master-stroke as he fitted the team's game plan well and he was also more of a physical player than many at West Perth. The team's token tough-guy in the late-1970s and 1980s was the Vietnam War veteran John Duckworth but with Duckie there was a humorous side to him (like Carlton's Peter "Percy" Jones and North Melbourne's Peter "Crackers" Keenan) and he tended to be primarily a ball-player and not one for king-hits off the ball.

Duckie meant a huge amount for player and fan morale; it could be argued that his return to the senior team at age 35 in 1985 was another reason behind the team's finals' appearance in that year although he did not himself play in the first semi-final versus Swan Districts which the club lost. Duckworth missed the last two qualifying games of the 1985 season due to the after-effects of swallowing a fish bone. He had not trained for three weeks as at the Monday of the lead-up week and had lost seven kilograms. He intended to resume training on the Thursday night before the first semi-final but ultimately he did not play. Duckworth surely must have enjoyed John Wynne's philosophy of having minimal pre-season training. He inspired the players and was worth much more to West Perth than his kick, marks, and handballs tally might suggest. The extremely charismatic and popular centre-half-forward Phil "Spock" Bradmore fits into the same category. Atkinson reports that Peter Menaglio won the Breckler Medal for club fairest-and-best player in 1984 while "Spock" Bradmore won the medal in the following year.

East Perth back then had a large number of fair-weather fans (as of course did West Perth) who would turn out in force for the big games and sit on the grassed scoreboard banks. Most of these have gone on to support one of Perth's AFL clubs. With East Perth there were certainly dumb-thug elements among the fair-weather army. As an example, when I went with Tim B., an East Perth supporter, to the big West Perth versus East Perth game at Leederville Oval on 26 August 1978, my father lagged behind us as he had to lock up all the car doors manually. As this was happening, Tim staged a mock fight with me on the

footpath. Just as in a cliché-ridden movie, an old panel van,
the vehicle of choice for mentally challenged thugs back in the
day, drove past Tim B. and me at that moment, and the driver
shouted out some brain-dead encouragement to the one wearing the
East Perth colours. East Perth's travelling supporters would sit
on the huge Leederville Oval scoreboard bank at West Perth home
games and, as mentioned, usually they did not wear the club
colours. This grass bank has largely disappeared today, in the
interests of the gentrification of the ground and the takeover
of the top part of the grass bank by the Town of Vincent, but it
can be seen in its full glory in the picture on page 219 of
Atkinson's book. On very big match days, most of the scoreboard
bank crowd would end up standing rather than sitting (at least
at the top and on the sides and edges).

East Perth had an organized cheer squad in the mid-1980s.
David Lockhart posted on the Lost WAFL Facebook page on 4
December 2013 to explain that he had been "the leader of this
rabble" from around 1982 to around 1988. He writes that the
cheer squad was funded by the East Perth club and had 40 members
at one point. He says his group knew the other cheer squads well
and participated in the combined State of Origin cheer squad a
few times. Our West Perth group did not know any of the members
of David Lockhart's cheer squad although Lockhart's group knew
Fat Pam's group which continued making the banners for the West
Perth players to run through into the 1984 season.

The East Perth fair-weather fans back in the day all
expanded significant effort trying to look macho and serious.
Ironically, Leederville Oval has now become East Perth's home
ground since the club was forced to leave Perth Oval for the
Perth Glory Soccer Club. It is indeed ironic that the East Perth
club, which prided itself on its macho, Aussie, tough-guy image
over the years, would have to leave its home ground for soccer,
the so-called sport of, to use the title of the late Johnny
Warren's autobiography, "fairies, wogs, and poofters" (yes,
Garlic Munchers). One might even want to refer to the concept of
"karma" here, a concept that many of the middle-aged, and upper-
middle-class "Buddhists" living in the now gentrified East Perth
suburb can probably relate to. As the Full Points Footy website
comments: "East Perth actually played its home matches at
Leederville [Oval] during season 2000 owing to Perth Oval being
consigned to the heretics, i.e. it was needed for the ineptly
named 'Perth Glory's' soccer fixtures".

I can remember attending the second last West Perth versus
East Perth game ever played at Perth Oval on Monday 1 June 1998.
I sat under the tin shed in the south-western corner, just to
the right of the main grandstand if you were looking across from
the scoreboard bank. There was an official crowd of 4,853

people, a very high crowd for the post-Fremantle Dockers era. East Perth actually won that day, 16.8 (104) to 8.10 (58), although West Perth made the grand final in that year only to lose it to East Fremantle. This 1 June 1998 match was the last WAFL game ever to be played at Perth Oval in front of a crowd exceeding three thousand people.

Despite East Perth vacating Perth Oval, West Perth supporters did not have the last laugh because East Perth then joined Subiaco as the new co-tenants of Leederville Oval! The ground has now become a yuppie, boutique style ground with most of the scoreboard wing gone (it can be viewed on Google Earth) as well as the around-the-ground seating including the cheer squad's seats behind the northern-end goal. In the general public parts of the ground only the seats in front of the tin shed in the north-west corner remain. Subiaco has built a tasteful new social club / grandstand in between the main grandstand and the tin shed which, if my memory serves me correctly, was home to a stepped section of gravel or concreted terracing (or an upwards sloping gravelled or concreted section) topped with a bar and / or a hot food caravan back in the 1980s (similar to the still-existing can bar terrace at Lathlain Perk). Despite all the changes, I still feel very much at home in the famous old ground. The old gates in the south-western corner have gone replaced by new Phil Matson Gates. It was somewhat cute and very politically correct to name these gates after Phil Matson who was a successful player and coach at both East Perth and Subiaco in the first half of the twentieth century. He can't have had many challengers. I can't imagine that the Alex Hamilton Gates or the Kevan Sparks Gates would have been deemed suitable names, these being the only two players I can think of from more recent years who played for both clubs. Oh, wait...The Peter Spencer Gates? I would like to see that!

The fact that Leederville Oval has become East Perth's home ground does not sit well with me, but, as Brian Atkinson pointed out in personal e-mail correspondence, once West Perth moved out any other club had the right to move in. Clearly Subiaco, after being forced out of its Subiaco Oval headquarters by the new power-brokers of football the Western Australian Football Commission (WAFC), perceived that a move effectively just down the street to Leederville Oval would pose the least threat to its identity as a name change would not be needed. Ironically and sadly, the only visible signs of red-and-blue I observed when I visited Leederville Oval on the peaceful and sunny winter morning of Wednesday 6 July 2011 was the colouring of the brand name of Medibank Private, the current sponsors of the ground, at the back of the old main grandstand. The ground is presently a mish-mash of colours, a genuine post-modern collage, as you can see the blue-and-black of East Perth only 20-metres away from the maroon-and-gold of Subiaco. However, despite this, I still love the dear old ground (as I also love Dorrien Gardens).

Evidence of the East Perth fair-weather fan mentality is the fact that the club's average attendances have been among the lowest of all WAFL clubs in the post-West Coast Eagles era. The so-called "dedicated" East Perth supporters of the early-1980s all quickly jumped ship at the first opportunity to support the new, artificial, corporate West Coast franchise. The concept of "loyalty" in Western Australian football since 1987 has been strained, muted, and bastardized, with some strange individuals following both West Coast and Fremantle in the AFL. Imagine people supporting both Manchester United and Manchester City or both the legendary Glasgow clubs Celtic and Rangers! Other West Australian football followers switched teams twice, once from their WAFL club to the West Coast Eagles in 1987 and once from the West Coast Eagles to the Fremantle Dockers in 1995.

A famous American sports fan turned commentator, Joe Benigno, wrote in his only partly tongue-in-cheek book Rules for New York Sports Fans that the number one "rule" for supporting sports in New York City is that you cannot have more than one team per sport, i.e. you cannot support both the Yankees and Mets in baseball or both the Giants and the Jets in American football or both the Knicks or Nets in basketball or two or more of the Rangers, Islanders or Devils in ice-hockey. This rule has always been modified in Australia where you were "allowed" to support one football team per competition in the 1970s and 1980s. For example, you could support Geelong, East Perth, and Port Adelaide or West Perth, Richmond, and Norwood (to name the three clubs that David Palm played for). This was unchanged in theory but became very confusing in practice after the West Coast Eagles joined the VFL/AFL as it was then "permitted" for you to leave your existing VFL/AFL team to support the Eagles which most, but by no means all, people did. Then in 1995 you were "permitted" to leave the Eagles to support the Dockers especially if you lived anywhere near the Fremantle area or if you had historic or family ties to either one of East or South Fremantle.

The Dockers, like baseball's New York Mets in relation to the Yankees and soccer's Melbourne City in relation to Melbourne Victory, became a team you supported if you didn't like the Eagles as much as a team you supported for its own sake. Philosophers Marx and Engels might have called the Mets and Dockers the anti-theses of the dialectical contradiction in that they only make sense in relation to the "big brother" that they always measure themselves up against.

Many people also abandoned their WAFL team, either in practice alone or in theory as well, to support the Eagles or Dockers. In 1987 some formally divorced their WAFL club while for others they simply ignored their old wife whilst becoming infatuated with their glamorous new blue-and-gold girlfriend (with those sexy eagles' wings)! This created an alarming situation where fans were not castigated for leaving their WAFL club to support an AFL club. In fact it was even regarded positively if you did so as the West Coast Eagles was mistakenly perceived by many to be a state team rather than just another club team which just happened to be Perth-based. Therefore, simply because the WAFL clubs and the AFL clubs were not in the same competition, it was acceptable to abandon your WAFL club in the post-West Coast Eagles era, and I always thought this was very disappointing and wrong-headed. Can you imagine supporters abandoning Manchester City, Newcastle United or West Ham United if they slipped out of the English Premier League? In fact Portsmouth FC recently attracted home crowds of around 16,000-18,000 people whilst playing in League Two (tier-four of the pyramid when viewed from the top). Furthermore, most Fremantle Dockers' supporters over the age of 30-35 used to be West Coast Eagles supporters making the "intensity" and "rivalry" of the early "Western Derby" played between West Coast and Fremantle ridiculous.

Tony Barker interviewed the business and football protagonists involved in the formation of the West Coast Eagles in 1986-87. The after-the-fact rationalizations, justifications, and profound analysis are interesting although we do not get an apology from any of those suited businesspersons who bled the Eagles dry in its first two years with conspicuous consumption and bad business decisions. These poor decisions include at the very least: (a) agreeing to pay a AUD4 million licence fee to the VFL up-front; (b) paying excessive amounts for the aging Ross Glendinning and the injury-prone Phil Narkle; (c) showing a distinct lack of ethics by pursuing contracted players Paul Harding and Gary Buckenara; (d) hiring two coaches Alexander and Todd without VFL/AFL coaching experience; and (e) inviting "corporate people" rather than "football people" on to the board.

Barker explores in depth the "personal politics" surrounding the births of West Coast in 1987 and Fremantle in 1995 and devotes three pages to Gerard Neesham's SWAFL. This is one of his book's clear strong points. Barker is rightly critical of the firing of coaches Ron Alexander and John Todd by West Coast in 1987 and 1989 and the manner in which those devious and sneaky "business transactions" were conducted and rationalized. However, in the main, Barker does not go beyond the assumption of nineteenth century scientific positivism that progress is always good, or, if not good, then at least "inevitable". Those who might scorn Marxism for alleged historical determinism all too quickly fall back on that word "inevitable" which aims, in effect, to make people unaccountable for their own choices and actions. The term suggests that the only reasonable choice available to us is to get behind the direction in which history is marching or engage in the futile task of trying to hold back the clock. Using this logic, then, Swan Districts' Bill Walker was and is a person "living in the past" whilst John Walker, Richard Colless, and the six pro-VFL WAFL club presidents become, for historians, virtuous (no matter what they actually did) because they were on "the side of history".

EAST PERTH v WEST PERTH
ROUND 16 (21 JULY) 1984
My personal 1984 season notes state as follows about the East Perth versus West Perth match at Perth Oval on 21 July 1984:

"East Perth 19.15 d West Perth 18.17. Perth Oval. Michael [B.] lost lens at Claisebrook Station. Huge record cheer squad – talked to [West Perth coach Dennis] Cometti before the match. Timeclock wasn't working – thrilling last quarter. Great games by [John] Gastev and [Derek] Kickett" [underlining in original].

Clearly the West Perth Cheer Squad had grown to its full and mature size by 21 July 1984 and, as mentioned previously, our group would swell at big away games as other West Perth fans would join us. This would include those who regularly sat in other sections of Leederville Oval (i.e. away from the cheer squad) at home games. When the cheer squad went to Perth Oval on 21 July 1984 we sat behind the southern-end goals just as we had previously done at Claremont Oval. There was no territorial invasion other than the physical entering of the ground.

The West Perth Cheer Squad had a large contingent that day (as my personal notes from 1984 record); the sun was lovely; and no-one disturbed the cheer squad members or insulted us. The East Perth Cheer Squad was behind the northern-end goals and so would not have met the West Perth Cheer Squad which sat at the southern-end goals after arriving from Claisebrook train station on the south-eastern side of the ground. The usual family groups of Aboriginal people that supported East Perth and sat under the trees near the back fence at the southern-end (Lord Street-end) were there that day but they gave the cheer squad not the slightest trouble nor the cheer squad them. West Perth was a multicultural club; when your lead rover is Fong and your lead ruck-rover is Menaglio and you have a Kickett and a Davis (two

Aboriginal players) on your team you would not want to entertain
a racist thought even if you were that way inclined. The grassed
bank behind the southern-end goals can be seen in a picture in
the Claremont history book which shows action from an East Perth
versus Claremont match played at the ground in the early-1970s.

As was typical of away games, the cheer squad members were
in a jovial, carnival mood all day which persisted even after
West Perth suffered a narrow loss. We all went back to
Claisebrook Station (where the lost contact lens incident
referred to in my season notes occurred) after the match in a
large group in order to journey back to Perth central train
station in the city-centre. The days at Claremont and Perth
Ovals were very similar: a large cheer squad group; fine
weather; a carnival atmosphere among the group; and a large
group claiming half a carriage on the train back into the city-
centre. We were possibly fortunate not to get into trouble with
opposing fans at Perth Oval. That trend would end with the cheer
squad's first and probably only visit to that most parochial of
WAFL grounds, Bassendean Oval, home of 1980s WAFL powerhouse the
Swan Districts Football Club.

The West Perth Cheer Squad (source: my personal 1984 WAFL season notes compiled during 1984):

Round 6 (5 May): West Perth versus South Fremantle at Leederville Oval. The cheer squad was formed on this day.

Round 10 (Monday, 4 June): West Perth versus East Perth at Leederville Oval: I watched this match with school friend Roy George.

Round 12 (23 June): West Perth versus Claremont at Subiaco Oval: Group members went into the club rooms after the game. The group members first met P.A. and R.T.

Round 13 (30 June): West Perth versus South Fremantle at Subiaco Oval. The group members sat with the unofficial West Perth supporter group called "Grandstand Falcons".

Round 14 (7 July): West Perth versus Swan Districts at Leederville Oval: The group introduced the "Cop That" banner to the cheer squad.

Round 15 (14 July): West Perth versus Perth at Leederville Oval. The group was "humbled by Perth cheer squad." The group took two flags from the club shed. In the city-centre after the match there was "raucous singing" by the group.

17 July (Tuesday): Western Australia (WA) versus Victoria State of Origin match at Subiaco Oval. Mike B. and I took the "Cop That" banner. I attended with school and neighbourhood friends Mike B., Paul B., Chad S., Roy G., Paul D., Gilby, Peter L., Wayne D., and Nick. This group of friends arrived at 9.20am. Gary Ablett Senior kicked eight goals for the losers. Best players for WA were Brad Hardie, Ross Glendinning, and Steve Malaxos. Dean Warwick (West Perth) failed to make the WA team. The West Perth Cheer Squad was invited to join the combined Perth-Claremont cheer squad, which was representing WA that day, in the grandstand but we declined.

Round 16 (21 July): West Perth versus East Perth at Perth Oval. Mike B. lost his contact lens at Claisebrook Station after the match. The group had a "huge record cheer squad". Group members talked to West Perth coach Dennis Cometti prior to the match. The official time-clock was not working. It was a "thrilling last quarter" with great games being played by West Perth players John Gastevich and Derek Kickett.

My personal WAFL season notes do not extend past Round 16 (21 July) 1984. There were only five WAFL home-and-away rounds played after this date. West Perth did not qualify for the 1984 final round series.

CHAPTER FOUR
WEST PERTH CHEER SQUAD: 1985

This chapter begins with a discussion of the cheer squad's
chants and its after-match ritual. I refer to the cheer squad's
chants at various points in this book. Unlike many soccer
supporters groups (such as Perth Glory's young Glory Fans
United) our chanting was not continuous throughout the match. As
the cheer squad always had around 15 to 20 people, and only on
one particular day at Subiaco Oval was there more than 50 (refer
to Chapter 1), the cheer squad lacked what Marsh terms "critical
density". According to Marsh a critical density is needed for a
group to begin to take on its own special dynamic where chants
are naturally synchronized and people can feel that their own
identity is submerged into that of the crowd. Marsh argues that
usually around 100 people are need before this very subjective
special group dynamic of "very marked unity" begins.

    The "West Perth clap clap clap" chant was uniformly used by
the cheer squad in response to West Perth goals. This or other
chants also occurred at various moments when the team was on an
energy or creative rush or, by contrast, when it needed some
encouragement. Chants usually ended after only a few repetitions
although the "West Perth clap clap clap" chant after goals went
on longer than the others. To some extent the volume, length,
and number of chants depended on both people's moods and the
state of the game. It should be mentioned that the cheer squad's
other favourite chants included "Phil Bradmore clap clap clap"
and "John Duckworth clap clap clap" and for Peter Menaglio
"Saint Peter clap clap clap" which was somehow very appropriate
given Menaglio's Italian background. Group members appreciated
and respected that West Perth was a multicultural club, we
revelled in it, and there was no obvious racism among the group.

    Group members would also sing "Johnnie Duckworth walks on
water / tralalalala lalalala" with group members' favourite West
Perth players' names being put into the chant. The reverse
(uncomplimentary) version of this chant was "Ronnie Boucher
walks on water / everybody knows that bullshit floats". It
should also be pointed out that the two "walks on water" chants
(the complimentary one and its reverse) were actually sung
rather than chanted. People may have been familiar with some of
the chants and songs from the days of Fat Pam's cheer squad. No
chants or songs were actually "written" in the sense of people
sitting down and consciously writing them. The cheer squad's
song about the inhabitants of the R.A. McDonald Stand at
Bassendean Oval, to be referred to later, was more complex than

the other songs / chants and it was an excellent and provocative one. It may have been inherited from Fat Pam's cheer squad. If not, I would like to know the origins of this particular song and whether other clubs' supporters sang it too.

The Grandstand Falcons used to sing "This Time (We'll Get It Right)", the original version of which was sung by the English national soccer team before the 1982 World Cup Finals. It was suitable for West Perth because, like England, it had been many years since our last success and the club had been a regular source of disappointment for the longsuffering fans. We generally only sang the song when in the presence of the Grandstand Falcons because it was "their" song.

In regards the after-match ritual, if the game was at Leederville Oval, the cheer squad members would run on to the field at the final siren, with flags waving in the air if it was a victory. Group members would also return the floggers promptly to the storerooms at the club. On some occasions group members might try to get into the dressing rooms if it had been a particularly impressive victory. Then we would celebrate the victory with the players and the other hardcore supporters. I can recall that on a few occasions the rooms were open to all supporters. My personal 1984 season notes, compiled during 1984, state that cheer squad members went into the dressing rooms after the Round 12 West Perth versus Claremont game played at Subiaco Oval won by West Perth 21.20 (136) to Claremont 9.14 (68). This was also the first game when the group was joined by P.A. and R.T. Brian Atkinson20 mentions that the coach of West Perth in 2011, the ex-Subiaco player Bill Monaghan, introduced a policy of opening up the change rooms after games regardless of the result.

Usually cheer squad members would kick their footballs kick-to-kick on the oval until it got dark. The group would remain largely intact during this time. The empirical fact that the cheer squad would remain intact during kick-to-kick and never formally join in with people from outside the cheer squad does support the proposition that the cheer squad was a "group-for-itself" rather than simply a "group-in-itself". Eight-year-old Michael ("Half") was always there on the oval with the group. His parents understood that this was a part of the group's routine and group members realized that his welfare remained the group's responsibility to a certain extent.

After it got dark cheer squad members would all leave the ground in a group of around 8 to 15 people and head for the train station (or the various bus stops if it was a home game). If it was an away game most of the complete group (excluding those six or seven people who came by cars such as Rohan, Courtney, Half, Ben, Rob, Tony, and Mario) would all get the train or bus back to the city-centre, still carrying the rolled-up flags. If it was an away game, a large group would head back by the train to the city-centre. The group would take over the back half of the bus or half a carriage on trains. The adrenaline and sweat from the kick-to-kick session would still be with the group members and the laughing and joking would fill the train carriage.

If it was a home game, only Mike B. and I and perhaps also Mike C. and Pete C. would take the Number 15 bus on Oxford Street back to Perth city-centre. The members of the "Balga group" (ranging from two to five people including P.A., R.T., Thommo, Thommo Junior, and Robbie) would walk eastward along Vincent Street by themselves to take their own bus back to the northern suburbs. (If it was an away game, the remaining people would say their goodbyes at the dark and cold Wellington Street bus terminal or at the Perth central train station.) Only Mike B. and I would then head south through the city-centre four blocks to St George's Terrace to catch the Number 105 bus back to Booragoon. Occasionally Mike B. and I might have stopped at Hungry Jack's or McDonald's but, if I recall correctly, the bus timing was tight and we had to walk rapidly through the city-centre. As with the Victorian cheer squads at Flinders Street Station in the 1970s and 1980s, Mike B. and I would sometimes encounter the Claremont or Perth cheer squads in the city-centre and we were on good terms with both of those groups. Both of those cheer squads understood the Victorian cheer-squad culture of camaraderie and mutual support outside the grounds. My 1984 season notes state that, after West Perth defeated Perth 17.19 (121) to 10.13 (73) at Leederville Oval on 14 July (Round 15), the West Perth cheer squad was involved in "raucous singing" in the city-centre! This was probably just Mike B. and me although Mike and Pete C. could have been there.

Without a doubt Swan Districts was the club of the early-1980s in the WAFL, i.e. the club which had and has the privileged position of being the Golden Club of the Golden Era. After being easy-beats for most of the late-1970s, with a bottom two position nearly assured, Swans, under the expert coaching of the disciplinarian John Todd, began a rapid ascent up the premiership ladder to the extent that the club played in (but lost) the 1980 grand-final against a brilliant Mal Brown coached South Fremantle team that included Basil Campbell; Brad Hardie; Stephen Michael; Joe McKay; the late Maurice Rioli; Tony Morley; and Benny Vigona. The Full Points Footy website comments as follows regarding the coaching style of John Todd:

"Whereas the best Western Australian teams have traditionally been renowned for producing highly-skilled, open, flowing football Todd tended to favour a more 'Victorian' approach. His teams were tough and determined, capable of brilliance, but more typically achieving victory by relentless running supplemented with substantial amounts of vigour. It is probably no coincidence that Todd went on to become the first coach to steer the West Coast Eagles into the finals as his style was eminently suited to the dog eat dog desperation of the [then] VFL".

The start of the Swans' era and the end of the Perth era

PERTH v SWAN DISTRICTS,
ROUND 3 (16 APRIL) 1979
I was actually there at that moment in 1979 when there was a symbolic "changing of the guard" between declining Perth (1976 and 1977 premiers and 1978 grand-finalists) and emergent Swans (premiers in 1982, 1983, and 1984 and 1980 grand-finalists). I was sitting high up in the visiting fans' section of the Lathlain Park grandstand with my late grandfather Mr. H.A.A. (1906-99) and his best mate Ernie Henderson on this day in April 1979. In a tense finish, the emergent Swans held on to win by four points to symbolize the end of the Perth era and the start of the Swans' era. East et al. report that the date was Monday 16 April 1979 and the final score was: Swan Districts 11.12 (78) defeated Perth 11.8 (74). The official attendance was 11,046. The picture on p. 166 of Dawson's book shows John Todd embracing his chairman of selectors Bob Manning at the end of this game. Dawson writes that: "There was palpable relief in John's face on the final siren, with Swans kicking only six points in the last term as Perth fought back from a three goal deficit".
   Although never a Swans' supporter, I was nonetheless caught up in the atmosphere of the game's tight finish, and I remember running down to the visiting team players' race (which was enclosed by just a wire-chain fence on both sides and over the top) to cheer the Swans' players as they left the ground. Years later, in the 1998 WAFL season when my grandfather was 92-years-old and I was 29, I took my grandfather to a Perth versus East Fremantle game at Lathlain Park. This was either the game on 4 April 1998 or the game on 8 August 1998. It took forever for me to help my grandfather walk up and down the main grandstand's steps. The late Mr. H.A.A. enjoyed the game (it was be his last ever game of football watched in the flesh) and especially the speed and skill of East Fremantle, the eventual premier team of that year. East Fremantle's team included the veteran Steve Malaxos whom my grandfather still remembered from his earlier stints at Claremont and West Coast. On a sunny day, the view from the top sections of the Lathlain Park grandstand is magnificent with the tree-tops in the middle distance, the blue

sky above, and the hills of the Darling Ranges as the backdrop. It is one of WAFL football's truly iconic views.

Swans in the early-1980s proved to be a master team and perhaps the last great WAFL dynasty of the pre-West Coast Eagles era to the extent that East Fremantle and Subiaco had their runs halted midstream by the formation of West Coast and most of the better players of both teams went on to join the Eagles. The West Coast Eagles effectively fielded an East Fremantle-Subiaco combined team in 1987.

Prime movers for Swans in the early-1980s were the future Essendon premiership player Leon Baker; Jon Fogarty; Don Holmes; Barry Kimberley; Don Langsford; the Aboriginal brothers Keith and Phil Narkle; Mike and Steve Richardson; and Brad Shine. The slightly more mercurial brother Phil Narkle later played for St Kilda and West Coast (when past his prime and dogged by injuries) and returned to win another premiership with Swans and John Todd (back from his two years at West Coast) in 1990. However, Phil's elder brother Keith never played VFL/AFL. Both brothers were excellent and fair players and widely admired by all WAFL club supporters. Keith was a mainstream of the Swans' team and, like the long-serving key-position players Stan Nowotny and Tom Mullooly, had been at the club since its miserable era of the late-1970s. A by then veteran Gerard Neesham helped Swans in the midfield in the early-1980s premiership years; he was still fast as well as physically tough and mentally disciplined. Neesham probably brought some of the self-confident East Fremantle winning culture over to Swans.

The Swans' 1982-84 premiership teams were perhaps not the most skilful although they were above average in this regard as well. Despite the presence of some brilliant players, it has to be said that "professional" or even "workmanlike" are adjectives that could have been used to describe many of the team's players, if not the team as a whole, in the early-1980s. John Todd gave his players mental toughness, resolve, courage, team spirit, and self-belief rivalled only perhaps in the WAFL by teams coached by Mal Brown and Gerard Neesham.

However, I believed that West Perth had a team capable of challenging Swans in 1985 as the Bassendean-based club was fast approaching the end of its great era. Most of its better premiership-era players had already left although, ominously for West Perth as it turned out, Garry Sidebottom had returned from his stint playing in Victoria.

Swans' fans re-gain control over every square-centimetre of
Bassendean Oval after West Perth invasion

SWAN DISTRICTS v WEST PERTH
BASSENDEAN OVAL, 1985
A trip to Bassendean Oval to play Swan Districts requires a long
train journey from the Perth city-centre on the ancient Midland
train line (opened 1 March 1881). Swan Districts is the most
remote from the city-centre of the six traditional WAFL clubs
which are not Fremantle-based. (Fremantle is often regarded as a
separate city in its own right.) By WAFL standards Bassendean is
a fairly compact ground with the outer grassy banks being less
wide and less high than those at East Fremantle Oval,
Leederville Oval (prior to its recent renovations) or Lathlain
Park. Like a soccer ground, all spectators are relatively close
to the play. The famous old stands hug the playing arena closely
and cast much of it in shadow in the late afternoons.

Since the formation of West Coast Eagles in 1987, "Swans"
has had a reputation, fiercely and jealously guarded, of being
the epitome of a traditional WAFL club. Bill Walker of Swan
Districts was one of only two WAFL club presidents to vote
against the entry of West Coast Eagles into the expanded VFL
(now AFL). Even the once vibrant Midland and Guildford
districts, at the centre of Swan Districts' geographic
heartland, retain a large proportion of historic buildings and
they seemed to have remained somewhat shielded from the
economic, social, and demographic changes that the rest of Perth
has experienced. The large Aboriginal population suggests to
some a more cultural, communal, and non-materialistic way of
life compared to other parts of the city. Bassendean Oval used
to be a fearsome place for visiting supporters; every corner of
it was claimed by some gang or other of Swans' supporters. Even
today, Swans attract larger home crowds than other WAFL clubs
and the compact nature of the ground makes a crowd of two to
three thousand mostly Swans' supporters still a fearsome
proposition for opposition fans and players.

Although there was and is a members' stand, the R.A.
McDonald Stand, in the ground's south-western corner, has always
contained vocal and hardcore Swan Districts' supporters of all
ages. The stand still contains such dedicated supporters today,
although nowadays there are empty seats during the main game. In
the WAFL's Golden Era patrons had to arrive long before the
start of the main game to be assured a seat in the McDonald
Stand (pronounced as if it had an extra "s" as in "McDonald's
Stand"). My late maternal grandfather Mr. H.A.A. and his best
mate Ernie Henderson always sat there, towards the top, in the

1970s and into the first half of the 1980s. I also sat with them there, on three or four occasions, although never when West Perth was the opponent.

On this most memorable day, most probably in 1985, the West Perth Cheer Squad headed out to Bassendean Oval, from Perth city-centre on the Midland train line. I cannot recall how many people met in the city-centre beforehand. There was probably a sub-group which got on at the city-centre and the long journey then magnified our good spirits, self-confidence, and camaraderie. West Perth had been performing well on the field in 1985 and a win would certainly not have been an unlikely outcome. The cheer squad was in celebration and party mood, travelling to a distant and remote ground at the far end of the metropolitan area. Many cheer squad members would not have gone to the ground before. It was the sort of the ground then, like West Ham United's Upton Park or Portsmouth's Fratton Park in the 1970s and 1980s, that you might avoid going to unless you had a large group and were in self-confident mood.

No part of Bassendean Oval is seemingly reserved for the away supporters (except perhaps the Bill Walker Stand which is located to the immediate right of the McDonald Stand when viewed from inside the playing arena). The McDonald Stand is only 20- or 30-metres from the southern-end goals. The northern-end goals are furthest from the train station so, logically, that was not the place for the away fans. The logic of the era was that visiting cheer squads would stay near the entrance that was closest to the train station so that meant the southern-end at Claremont Oval and the southern-end at Perth Oval. It is like when invited to someone's home you stay in the visitor's couch in the living-room and don't go to the bedrooms! Lathlain Park was and is different because the main entrance affords easy access to both goals. However, since Nick's Perth FC Cheer Squad had claimed the northern- or city-end goals at Lathlain Park, away team cheer squads in the mid-1980s would sit at the southern-end goals out of respect. I argue that, although fraternal camaraderie was the norm among cheer squads throughout Australia, based on the Victorian model, there was still an "illusion of violence" since, if the rules of protocol or politeness were not followed by everyone, the mood could turn ugly and many cheer squad members were from working-class or lumpenproletariat backgrounds.

I can recall our West Perth group this day entering what were then the most popular gates of the oval, in the south-west corner closest to Success Hill train station, with the giant flags. In the environment of Bassendean Oval, these flags stood out like a sore thumb. Swans' fans then had a dour and austere culture where you would not wear club colours. Anything slightly

showy was frowned upon as not befitting this working-class
district far removed from the city-centre. Furthermore, Swans'
colours are black-and-white; the cheer squad's red-and-blue
jerseys and flags stood out like the first year of colour
television. People probably thought that we were show-offs and
smart-arses. We took the path of least resistance and set
ourselves up behind the southern-end goals. The group's flags
and banners were right there in front of the line of sight of
the McDonald Stand's inhabitants around 25-metres away. The
heritage-protected ground is largely unchanged today. One
picture on the WAFL Golden Era website at
waflgoldenera.blogspot.com shows the McDonald Stand as viewed
from the southern-end goals while another picture shows the
opposite view (the southern-end goals as viewed from the
McDonald Stand) (date of pictures: 12 July 2011).

The cheer squad was chanting its usual chants that day but
with perhaps unusual venom. There had been animosity between
West Perth supporters and Swan Districts' coach John Todd since
Todd left West Perth's Brian Adamson out of a Western Australian
combined state team in 1975. This animosity had then followed
Todd across from East Fremantle to Swan Districts. Dawson writes
as follows about the relationship between Swans and West Perth
during the 1980s: "The feud was always publicly denied, but
continued into the 1980s and all Swans-West Perth games were
well-attended with many fiery incidents, off and on the field".
Swans' record home ground attendance remains today the 22,350
people who watched Swans play West Perth on 10 May 1980 (Round
6).

It may have been the "Ronnie Boucher walks on water /
everybody knows that bullshit floats" chant that made the Swan
Districts' fans increasingly upset on this particular day in
1985. (Ronnie Boucher was Swan Districts' strong aggressive
ruckman of the era.) Swan Districts had no recognized or
organized cheer squad then but generally cheer squads accept
each other's chants as just part of the job description and not
to be taken seriously. I doubt very much whether the West Perth
Cheer Squad would have been offended by, for example, the Perth
Cheer Squad's chants. Much more dangerous than opposing cheer
squads are the disorganized fans. The McDonald Stand was an
intimidating place in that era and our cheer squad was insulting
Swans' players and showing off its vibrant red-and-blue colours
directly in front of their noses. The cheer squad also had its
famous song, sung to the tune of the classic children's song
"Old McDonald had a Farm": "Old McDonald had a stand/ eyie eyie
oh / and in that stand was full of pigs / eyie eyie oh". Of
course the cheer squad members all thought this song was very
funny and we sang it repeatedly and at maximum volume. It may

have been inherited from Fat Pam's cheer squad. If not then I do not know who actually coined it.

Around three-quarter time during the main game, we saw that a group of around eight to ten Aboriginal youths, around the group members' ages or slightly older, had very quietly surrounded us and taken up strategic seating positions just outside the group on all three sides. This Aboriginal group began to make intimidating comments including that they would beat our group members up after the game. The Aboriginal group members wore no club colours but they were very clearly Swans' supporters. They must have been offended by the West Perth flags and chanting. Our West Perth Cheer Squad watched the game much more diligently and stopped playing up to and taunting the inhabitants of the McDonald Stand. I could tell that our group members were apprehensive. Aboriginal gang culture and the culture of the suburbs around Bassendean Oval were not well known to any of the group. None of us had any reputation in the area that we could call upon whereas people like Thommo, Courtney, and Robbie were widely known and liked in large swathes of the northern suburbs and P.A. was the King of Balga. It was the classic away fans scenario.

We all began to watch the game much more diligently and talk among ourselves; we adopted a much lower profile. We became just normal fans rather than a cheer squad as such. Even the noisiest members became quiet which was very remarkable. People became grossly absorbed in the match, looked straight ahead, and quietly conversed in their twos and threes. This was partly a strategic act and partly a sub-conscious switch to the self-preservation mode. The chanting mostly stopped although I am sure that we still waved the flags after West Perth goals. One had to literally fly the flag. If we want some theorization of the cheer squad's behaviour self-modification, we might cite Peter Marsh who writes in Aggro: the Illusion of Violence that:

"[w]e can instantly recognize dominant or submissive stances in other people and we frequently employ them ourselves ... Adopting a submissive posture is the clearest way in which ... a person ... can signal that he has had enough and thus avoid serious injury".

When the game ended, or possibly five or ten minutes prior to that, the West Perth Cheer Squad looked around and they saw that the Aboriginal group had disappeared. I do not think that anyone even saw or heard them leave. Our West Perth group had passed some kind of test. Possibly the Swan Districts' group had decided that we were "good guys at heart" or possibly they had just lost interest in confrontation or had somewhere to go straight after the match. Swans' on-field victory that day might possibly have been seen by the Aboriginal group as having been vindication enough for them (as Mike B. today claims21).

Like the London Teddy Boys who menacingly surrounded Desmond Morris and his wife in a Camden Town cafe in 1957 but then paid the couple's bill and left with a friendly greeting, the Swan Districts group had reinforced territorial dominance by Swans' fans over Bassendean Oval, including the seats behind the southern-end goals, without resorting to actual violence. It must be said that the late Mr. R.A. McDonald does indeed have a stand and that stand is full of fine, up-standing citizens. Marsh explains further as follows: "When men enter into aggressive confrontations with each other, the object of the exercise is not killing but preservation of dominance relations, the defence of particular space or access to basic resources".

The Swan Districts versus West Perth match was probably either the 19.14 (128) to 15.12 (102) Swans' victory on 8 April 1985 (attendance 10,500) or the 22.12 (144) to 21.16 (142) Swans' victory on 20 July 1985 (attendance 9,462). It was probably the first one of these as I remember that interest and atmosphere had drained out of the match prior to the last 10 or 15 minutes. One interesting fact is that West Perth defeated Swans five times out of nine during Swans' premiership years of 1982-84. By contrast, in 1985, when Swans were not among the top two teams and West Perth made the finals series, Swans defeated West Perth three times out of three in the regular season games and one more time in the first semi-final. It is certainly hard to explain this. Such are the vagaries of football.

This event at Bassendean Oval's southern-end goals was a near-miss for the West Perth Cheer Squad and the group members probably learned a lesson to be somewhat less cocky, more respectful, and more circumspect in hostile away territory. It must be pointed out that the cheer squad members never viewed this encounter as any sort of "racial war" – our group was multicultural and had a multicultural ethos. For example, R.T. from Tuart Hill was an ethnic Chinese and the brothers Tony and Mario were of Italian ethnicity. In fact West Perth supporters have long been referred to by the racist tag of "Garlic Munchers" (especially by East Perth fans). This tag emerged because of the large southern-European support base which was attracted to the club in the immediate post-World War II period.

Ronnie Boucher flexes his muscles in front of the West Perth
Cheer Squad

WEST PERTH v SWAN DISTRICTS
ROUND 14 (7 JULY) 1984
On another occasion, this time at Leederville Oval in 1984, the
West Perth Cheer Squad incurred the wrath of Swan Districts'
ruckman Ron Boucher. No opposition player ever reacted to the
cheer squad or responded to it, other than Boucher, in those
years from 1984-86. The West Perth Cheer Squad felt that Boucher
was an unpleasant character. He was out-of-place in the great
Swans' teams of the early-1980s as he resembled a country
footballer from thirty years previously. The Full Points Footy
website writes about Ron Boucher as follows although other
sources confirm that Boucher did play on into the 1984 season
although he missed the losing grand-final side:

"Recruited from North Albany, Ron Boucher made his league debut
with Swan Districts in 1971. Extremely powerfully built at 192cm
and 102kg, he used his strength to awesome effect, most notably
during Swans' halcyon period under John Todd in the early
1980s. He was one of his team's best in the losing grand final
against South Fremantle in 1980, and was a key contributor to
premiership wins in 1982-3, despite having to battle for much of
the time with persistent niggling injuries. He was equally
effective as a knock ruckman or a strong marking forward, and
was selected in a forward pocket in Swan Districts' official
'Team of the Century'.
Ron Boucher played 190 games for Swan Districts between 1971 and
1983 [sic], as well as representing Western Australia. He won
the club's fairest and best award in his penultimate season".

The West Perth Cheer Squad had a reverse (uncomplimentary)
version of its "walks on water" chant reserved for opposition
players as follows: "Ronnie Boucher walks on water / everybody
knows that bullshit floats". P.A., Mike C., Pete C., and Thommo
especially thought that this chant was just hilarious. There was
also an alternative, negative chant variant "Ronnie Boucher woo-
hoo" and at the last syllable people would raise their right
arms to around face height and then move their open right hands
in downwards motion in front of their raised, stiff wrists. I am
certain that readers will be aware of the particular hand
gesture which is being referred to here. As an ex-West Perth
player and one the club should really have held on to the late
Chris Stasinowsky also received this treatment from the cheer
squad when he played for Perth in 1985 and 1986.

Mike B. recounted to me one 1984 Leederville Oval incident involving Boucher which had failed to rise to the top of my memory and which had not appeared in the first draft of this book. This is a fiery incident relating to West Perth versus Swans matches in the 1980s which has not previously been made public. According to Mike B.22, on this day at Leederville, Boucher became upset by our cheer squad's chants and he walked up to where Mike B. and I were seated, leaned forward over the boundary fence, grabbed Mike B. by his West Perth replica jersey, and demanded to know: "What did you f***ing say?" In deep shock, Mike B. managed to stammer: "I'm really sorry, Mr. Boucher". In an interesting postscript to this story, Mike B. mentioned that years after this Leederville Oval incident he contested an arm-wrestling bout against Boucher in Broome which was the town where Boucher was then living. To no-one's surprise Boucher ultimately beat all other contestants and won the contest.

There is one last chant of our West Perth Cheer Squad which I have not discussed. This chant is probably the most controversial used by the cheer squad and so it should be left to last. If you ask me now which actions, if any, I regret I would answer "this chant in particular". As mentioned, South Fremantle had a contingent of brilliant Aboriginal players in the early-1980s and West Perth had two great Aboriginal players in Derek Kickett and Ron Davis. Another Aboriginal player with great talent and flair was half-forward Lindsay Henry who played five games for West Perth in the 1988 season. One of South Fremantle's greats was wingman Benny Vigona, a member of the 1980 premiership side and the 1979 and 1981 losing grand-final teams. Vigona polled seven votes in the 1984 Sandover Medal Count, half as many as scored by the equal fourth-place getters Laurie Keene (Subiaco) and Peter Menaglio (West Perth). The Full Points Footy website writes as follows about the great Benny Vigona:

"After commencing his senior career with St Marys, where he won back to back best and fairest awards, Benny Vigona moved to South Fremantle in 1977 and rapidly developed into one of the WANFL competition's most exciting talents. Initially used mainly either on a wing or at half forward, he boasted sublime ball skills, explosive pace, and a penchant for the spectacular. Later in his career he was shifted to a half back flank with considerable success, reinforcing his undoubted ability with a newfound consistency in the process. In a decade with South, Vigona amassed close to 200 league games and represented Western Australia on 4 occasions".

The West Perth Cheer Squad had a chant of "Benny's got a Vigona!" Obviously the chant was only used at games against South Fremantle. I do not know the origin of this chant but everyone thought that it was funny. It may have come from Fat Pam's cheer squad, Grandstand Falcons or some other group of West Perth support. Fortunately, there is little chance that Benny himself heard the chant as he was a midfielder and the cheer squad always sat behind the goals. Marsh provides some theoretical commentary regarding the need to "feminize" one's opponents as a part of "aggro" and "the illusion of violence":

"The examination of the football [hooligan] aggro phenomenon revealed a very important process. It showed that in the context of the striving for manly dominance a highly strategic weapon was the system of insults which served to demasculinize one's rivals. Making them appear homosexual or, better still, feminine was part and parcel of this particular manifestation of aggro".

Was this a racist chant? It certainly represents a deliberate attempt to "feminize" a rival star Aboriginal player. The chant opportunistically takes advantage of a surname that obviously can be used quite easily as the principal ingredient for toilet humour. I do not personally think that it was a racist chant as if a white footballer had happened to have had a similar sounding surname then the chant would still have been used. Although this is subjective I can recall no animosity around the use of the chant in terms of tone or accompanying chit-chat – the chant was just a form of comic relief. There was much more venom involved in chants about Swan Districts and that club's players such as Ronnie Boucher. South Fremantle was not a major rival of West Perth in the 1980s. Nonetheless, it is a chant that I definitely regret. Aboriginal players do not need to bear any additional burdens or stresses whilst on the playing field. It is easy to excuse the chant by saying that these were less politically correct times but, then again, I have already discussed my dislike of the unambiguously racist "Garlic Munchers" tag as applied to West Perth supporters by East Perth fans.

Interestingly, Atkinson documents that, in February 2004, a group of West Perth members began calling themselves the "Garlic Munchers" to differentiate themselves from other members in terms of their views about the adoption of "Joondalup Falcons" as the club's trading name. This is a similar situation to those Greek-Australians who voluntarily adopted the "wog" tag in the popular early-1990s stage-show Wogs Out of Work (created by Nick Giannopoulos and Simon Palomares) or those African-Americans who have voluntarily used the word "nigger" in relation to

themselves. This behaviour can be seen as altering power
relations by turning the abusive word into a term of endearment
or even empowerment when used by a certain group of people in
certain ways and at certain times of their own choosing. It is a
very political act as it takes over the discursive space and
provides new opportunities for the fight against racism whilst
also being used to further group cohesion and self-identity. The
barrier between "insiders" and "outsiders" is retained but it is
now turned into something positive and powerful from the
viewpoint of the group using the stigmatized name.

Enter Garry Sidebottom, destroyer of West Perth dreams

FIRST-SEMI FINAL 1985
WEST PERTH v SWAN DISTRICTS
SUBIACO OVAL, 31 AUGUST
West Perth earned a rematch against Swan Districts in the 1985
first semi-final played on 31 August 1985 at Subiaco Oval. In
those days there was a grassed northern bank at the city-end and
there was concrete terracing all along the Roberts Road or
eastern side of the ground. These were the general admission
ticket areas back then. In that era, for every final apart from
the grand-final, there was no need to pre-book tickets at
Subiaco Oval unless you wanted grandstand seating. In those days
semi-finals would attract between 20,000 and 35,000 people and
the oval itself could accommodate close to 50,000. Nowadays
grand-finals struggle to attract even the type of crowds that
semi-finals attracted in the WAFL's Golden Era.
    In the newspapers leading up to the game the media
columnists were split fairly evenly in terms of which team they
thought would win the game. Swan Districts' Garry Sidebottom was
widely and correctly perceived to be the wild-card who, on a
good day, could single-handedly destroy West Perth up forward
which is exactly what happened. West Perth also suffered from
Menaglio being out injured; Duckworth not having recovered from
an absence caused by the after-effects of swallowing a fish
bone; and, although Comerford, Fong, and Michalczyk did play,
they were well below their bests as a result of carrying
niggling injuries into the game from the qualifying rounds.
Swans' tough centreman Tony Solin had also been expected to miss
the game on the Monday of the lead-up week but he returned to
play a very strong game. Rogers and the veteran Murnane missed
the last qualifying game versus a lacklustre Claremont, but
Murnane was expected to return for the semi-final and be able to
slot in well to replace the injured Menaglio. As it turned out
Murnane did play but he was not listed in any commentator's
best-players list. Meanwhile, Rogers' match statistics of one

mark, zero kicks, and two effective handballs suggest that he was still incapacitated.

On first semi-final day, 1985, Mike B. and I took an early morning bus from Booragoon to the city-centre and then the train to West Leederville station. The West Perth Cheer Squad had arranged to meet at the Subiaco Road entrance gates, in the north-east corner of the ground, rather than at the more crowded Roberts Road gates in the south-east corner. Group members had planned beforehand to get tickets on the day and to be first in the gates when they opened which must have been fixed at about 8am or 9am. The cheer squad members needed to be early to claim a seat immediately behind the fence on the two rows of wooden seats in front of the grassed bank. Mike C. and Pete C. were ahead of Mike B. and me in line when we arrived. Mike and Pete were carrying their red-and-blue flags and wearing their long-sleeve West Perth replica jerseys. I can't recall if they already had their tickets and were waiting for Mike B. and me outside the line or whether they were simply there already ahead of us in the queue. We all obtained our general admission tickets quickly and we (others may have been there too by then) were near the front of the waiting crowd when the gates opened.

The general admission tickets entitled you access to the grassed northern bank and to the concrete terracing but not to the grandstands. As was the practice in that era, our cheer squad members sprinted up and then down the grassed bank when the gates opened and claimed a section of seats directly behind the fence, sufficient to accommodate the core 15 people we were expecting for the game. The early arrivals claimed around eight spots on each of the first two wooden seat rows as had been agreed by everyone the week before at the final home-and-away game. The cheer squad sat in the north-east corner of the ground, directly behind the fence, in around the same place as Perth supporters placed a "Chris Mitsopoulos" fence banner during the 1977 grand-final.

Cheer squad members settled down to a long day of watching the early colts and reserves games which, coincidentally, all involved West Perth. The regular core group members all arrived, one by one and in twos and threes, and were offered seats in the group's new "reserved" section. The crowd in the grassed banked area built up steadily throughout the day. By starting time for the main game most people seated on the grassed bank had given way to people standing up. In that era the bars and the food stands were located right at the top of the grassed bank at the city-end. No group member drank beer at games which, in hindsight, is somewhat surprising as several people were 18-years-old by August 1985 (see Appendix A).

Cheer squad members planned to enjoy the day; again there was a carnival atmosphere, but the group had been metaphorically sobered up by the recent encounter with the Swan Districts' fans at Bassendean Oval so people were careful to avoid trouble. It was always uncertain which team the bulk of the crowd nearest you would support at finals games and, if you arrived at the ground very early, you might later find yourself surrounded by opposition supporters. Therefore, it was wiser to restrain your behaviour before the start of the main game.

We had all had previous experiences of West Perth losing final round matches. The team had entered the final-four, but not made the grand-final, in 1976, 1977, and 1978, and again in 1982 in Dennis Cometti's first year of coaching. Group members were mostly too young to have properly experienced the 1975 premiership win; on this day in 1985 the core group, excluding Ben, Rob, Tony, Half, Mario, and Thommo Junior, ranged in age from 15 to 19 so in 1975 this core group would have been aged from five to nine. Group members had learned not to have high hopes of West Perth come finals' time. To be honest people all expected a loss but we would have loved a win. In the end West Perth was duly defeated by Swan Districts in the first semi-final of 1985, 24.14 (158) to 19.12 (126) in front of an official attendance of 26,508 people. The team had not been humiliated but I do remember clearly that the result was never in serious doubt this day. The result did not surprise the cheer squad members as all of us were West Perth fans of the drought era (to use Brian Atkinson's term)!

Garry Sidebottom was unbeatable with his nine goals, the equal record highest score by any footballer in a WAFL final round match. Dawson writes that: "[Swans' rover Barry] Kimberley played the kick behind the play role to perfection when West Perth had the breeze, ensuring Swans path to the preliminary final". West Perth's losing score of 19 goals was commendable and, according to Atkinson, on most days would have been good enough to win the game.23

A look at the scoring records suggest that West Perth in 1985 suffered from the lack of a regular full-forward with the club's on-ball and half-forward-line running players bobbing up to kick much of the team's scores. Mark Stephens (27 games, 1982, 1984-86) was named in The West Australian newspaper to play full-forward in the first semi-final but he kicked no goals or points and may not even have played. Top scorers for the day for West Perth were centre-half-forward Phil Bradmore with 4.1 and Derek Kickett with 4.1. Running players were the only other West Perth men to kick more than one goal with the remaining multiple goal scorers being Darren Bewick 3.1, Corry Bewick 2.2, Les Fong 2.2, and Peter Murnane 2.0. Incredibly no recognized full-forward was recruited by West Perth for the 1986 season and West Perth fans had to endure the ignominy of watching West Perth reject Mick Rea perform splendidly for Perth in both 1985 and 1986 playing as a conventional lead-mark-kick full-forward. On first semi-final day 1985, the presence of full-forward Sidebottom and Swans' mental toughness honed by years of successful finals' campaigns were clearly the two main differences between the teams.

In the end, Swan Districts failed to progress further beyond the preliminary final in 1985, and Ron Alexander's East Fremantle defeated Haydn Bunton Junior's Subiaco by a mere five points in the grand-final. I watched the grand-final not with the cheer squad but with my father and grandfather seated in the middle-tier of the three-tier grandstand at the western-end of Subiaco Oval (following a family tradition rather than a cheer squad tradition this time around). I can remember walking back to our car after the game, heading back into Subiaco proper, and we stopped a few times to let my grandfather take short rests sitting on little brick walls and similar. After West Perth had been eliminated, we all understood that the cheer squad's duties and commitments were over for the year.

Ironically, to pour salt into the wounds, West Perth defeated eventual premiers East Fremantle two out of three times in the 1985 home-and-away rounds. None of the cheer squad members would have regarded East Fremantle as clear favourites had West Perth gone on to encounter the Sharks in the 1985 grand-final. West Perth probably had the Moss Street-based club's measure. Football is made up of vagaries, trivia, and ironies such as this. In fact, from 1976-86, the pre-West Coast Eagles part of the drought era, West Perth generally had a strong record against the eventual premiers. Most West Perth supporters believed that the team could beat anyone on its day, throughout the drought era, with the possible exception of the 1979 season. However, from 1976 through to 1985, West Perth was always choked or outplayed or outmuscled in those final round matches it did manage to play in. It might have been a nerves problem and /or a matter of self-belief. West Perth was up against highly professional and disciplined teams coached by legendary and expert WAFL coaches including Ken Armstrong (Perth); Mal Brown (South Fremantle and Perth); Haydn Bunton Junior (Subiaco); and John Todd (Swan Districts).

Those hardcore West Perth supporters of the drought era were not foolish enough to fail to see a pattern at work. The team clearly ran on enthusiasm, confidence, emotion, and passion during those years. Whereas most other clubs started slowly under a new coach only to reach first the finals, then to lose a grand-final, and then finally to win one, West Perth peaked in the first year of a new coach and then the trend was downhill until the next new coach was brought in! As examples of the normal course of events at other clubs, Perth lost in 1974 but won in 1976 and 1977; East Perth lost in 1976 but won in 1978; South Fremantle lost in 1979 but won in 1980; Swans lost in 1980 only to win in 1982, 1983, and 1984; East Fremantle lost in 1977 but won in 1979 and later lost in 1984 but won in 1985; whilst Subiaco lost in 1985 but won in 1986. Later on VFL/AFL club West Coast, famously, lost in 1991 but won in 1992 and 1994. The principle even applied to pre-drought West Perth when it lost in 1973 but won in 1975. It was certainly true, in that era, that "you had to lose a grand-final before you could win one" and this adage became wise advice in Western Australia not only for football but for life in general. Dawson also, referencing this period in WAFL history, refers to what he terms "an old football adage", i.e. "you must lose one to understand what is needed to win one".

However, departing from the normal pattern at the other WAFL clubs, West Perth won in 1975 in Graham Campbell's first year; reached the finals in 1982 in Dennis Cometti's first year; and reached the finals again in John Wynne's first year in 1985. However, West Perth failed to make the finals in Cometti's second and third years (1983 and 1984); and again in Wynne's second year (1986). Even in the immediate post-West Coast era the club made the finals under George Michalczyk in his first season in 1989 only to be wooden-spooners for his next two seasons.24 The theory that this constituted a unique West Perth pattern was a fairly convincing one although, in all of the years, there were a host of other factors that no doubt could also be used to explain the various rises and falls. It seems that the West Perth playing group became enthusiastic under a new coach but then became bored and lackadaisical by the coach's second year. It didn't seem to be a very mature response to the outside observer.

CHAPTER FIVE
WEST PERTH CHEER SQUAD: 1986

The Perth Football Club's cheer squad, operating under the
capable hands of the suave "metrosexual" Nick, was the leading
cheer squad among the WAFL clubs in 1984 and 1985. My personal
1984 season notes, compiled during 1984, state: "Humbled by
Perth cheer squad" at the West Perth versus Perth match at
Leederville Oval on 14 July 1984. Being "humbled" here must
refer to the respective size of the two groups and the
respective numbers of flags, floggers, and banners both groups
had on display. There was a combined Perth-Claremont cheer squad
which represented WA at the 17 July State of Origin match versus
Victoria so clearly these were the two leading cheer squads in
1984. It was at the Lathlain Park social club rooms that all the
cheer squads met one night (probably in 1984) to discuss the
making of the banner for the upcoming state game. I do not
recall how the West Perth Cheer Squad contributed to the making
of the banner but our members all appreciated the warm and
fraternal atmosphere generated by the host club and the host
club's cheer squad. I am very sure that Nick had had some prior
experience with a Victorian cheer squad as he had a clear
understanding of how a cheer squad should be organized and cheer
squad ethics. For Lathlain Park home games in 1984 and 1985 they
always had a large and fine-looking group of people with flags,
banners, and floggers congregated behind the northern- or city-
end goals. Even today there is a visual reminder of this cheer
squad at Lathlain Park - the wooden seats behind the city-end
goals are still painted red-and-black in memory of the days and
years in which Nick's cheer squad occupied those benches.

An emergent Perth brings West Perth to heel under the sun at
Lathlain

PERTH V WEST PERTH,
ROUND 1 (29 MARCH) 1986
I can recall only one game the West Perth Cheer Squad attended
at Lathlain Park, the first game of the 1986 season. The game
was played on the Saturday of the opening split round on 29
March 1986 and West Perth drew Perth with both sides scoring
13.15 (93). Although Perth started very strongly and led for
most of the match West Perth opened up a seven point lead in the
last quarter until Perth hit back to secure the draw. The match
was played on the same day as only one other game, a replay of
the 1985 grand-final between East Fremantle and Subiaco (won

this time by Subiaco 18.9 (117) to 12.11 (83)). The official attendance at Lathlain Park for the Perth versus West Perth match is recorded as 8,121 fans. Already by 1986 WAFL crowds had begun to trend slowly downwards. In the late-1970s or early-1980s, on a fine Saturday such as this one, the opening day of a split round and the opening day of the season, you would have expected the crowd to be above the ten thousand mark or even above twelve thousand.

I recall that the West Perth Cheer Squad had a very large group present; and we sat behind the southern-end goals with Perth's cheer squad congregated behind the northern- or city-end goals. A picture on the WAFL Golden Era website (taken 2 July 2011) shows the area behind the southern-end goals in modern times but before the redevelopment of the ground commencing in 2016. The West Perth Cheer Squad probably didn't meet the Perth Cheer Squad on this day in 1986 as the main entrance gates at Lathlain Park were positioned only around 30-metres to the north of the main grandstand, on the western side of the oval, and you could reach the southern-end goals by walking through the undercover passageway located underneath the grandstand. This day in 1986 was a very hot day, as you might expect from March in Perth, and people had their long-sleeved replica West Perth jerseys tied around their waists. Everyone was wearing tee-shirts but most people still wore the obligatory tight black or blue jeans rather than shorts. The cheer squad members were all classic 1980s Bogans except for Mike B, Courtney, and Rohan H., our football "casuals". P.A., for one, was never seen in shorts, which is probably something to be thankful for. R.T. and the C. brothers also never wore shorts and the same also applied for Thommo and me.

The cheer squad members were all happy to see each other again after a long summer without contact. It was as if everyone had put in a major mental effort to keep the cheer squad alive in some part of their minds, conscious and subconscious, over the summer. The cheer squad was the kind of organization which could survive only based on collective memories and collective willpower because there was nothing else holding it together. The cheer squad had no official name or headquarters or leaders or business cards or stationery or telephone number.

No-one very much minded that this game was a draw. Although Perth had not been a powerhouse, up until that point in the 1980s, Mal Brown was now in his second year at the helm as coach of Perth and people naturally expected that he would continue to inject discipline, purpose, and soul into the team as he had done previously at South Fremantle. The cheer squad members hoped that West Perth could continue on in 1986 in the same style as in 1985 and secure at least a final-four position.

However, we were drought era West Perth youth and I do not think that anyone really expected a premiership! East Fremantle and Subiaco were both expected to be strong teams again in 1986. However, to balance this, it did appear to be the end of a great era at Bassendean Oval as most of Swans' premiership era stars had moved on or had retired. John Todd was effectively back where he had started at Swans ten years previously although people's continued confidence in his ability to work miracles with a depleted squad had never been higher.

I can remember the cheer squad members staying out on the playing field at Lathlain Park until dark or near-dark kicking footballs around among the cheer squad group. All or nearly all of the core members of the group were there this day at Lathlain Park in March 1986 with the possible exception of Mike B., who may not have rejoined the group at all that year. By 1986 I was no longer meeting Mike daily at high-school. After the cheer squad members had exhausted all the possibilities of kick-to-kick, we walked together as a gang back to the Victoria Park train station. On this March day in 1986 everyone had to travel north-west on the Armadale train line back to the city-centre and then most people would transfer to their various buses to take them back to the northern suburbs. The Clarkson train-line to the northern suburbs was still some years away from being built.

I can recall that it was already dark by the time the group members reached the train station. It must have been as late as 7.30pm or 8pm as 29 March is closer to summer proper than to winter proper. I then decided, on the spur of the moment, not to cross over to the western side of the track to catch the city-bound train. Instead I stayed with the much smaller group of people waiting to take the train in the south-easterly direction towards Armadale. I remember talking with some Aboriginal boys at the Victoria Park station and telling them that I lived near Applecross and knew "Raymond Davies" who was the only recognizable Aboriginal person at high-school and who was a good friend of my mate Roy "The Spoon" George. In fact I had probably only ever talked to Raymond once meaning that I was a "namedropper" which you really had to be at high-school to survive. I had left high-school and was at university by this time. The Aboriginal boys welcomed the name, or maybe just my friendliness. There was a good atmosphere there. I waved and shouted across the track to the other West Perth cheer squad members on the other side before people's respective trains took them away into the darkness.

I decided that I would visit my grandparents who lived within walking distance of the Beckenham station further down the track on the Armadale line. This was a totally spur of the moment decision. They were both very surprised to see me standing on the front porch in the semi-darkness carrying my rolled-up West Perth flag. Years later, after they had both passed away, I lived in that house for two years (October 2002 – January 2004) before moving to New South Wales for work.

I have mentioned elsewhere that this Lathlain Park match was the last time the West Perth Cheer Squad existed in recognizable form. It was like the saying that it is always darkest before the dawn. It was as if the collective mental effort involved in keeping the group together psychologically, or in other words in people's head space, over the summer off-season (six months long in Perth) had simply been too exhausting. Once the key people stopped expending this mental effort the group just ceased to exist. It was quite remarkable or even magical.

I can only recall one subsequent 1986 game at Leederville Oval. The cheer squad may have kept the flags and floggers in action for a few more home games but I personally regard the Round 1 Lathlain Park match as being the last game for the cheer squad. In what was a remarkable outcome, the cheer squad's first game together was a drawn match (5 May 1984) and its last game together (29 March 1986), nearly two calendar years later, was also a drawn match. No-one made a deliberate decision to end the group as far as I can recall. I had become a dedicated student after entering university and I may simply have stopped putting in maximum effort to keeping the group going. Mike B. was probably in the same position in 1986 in terms of his mind drifting elsewhere. I can't even remember if Mike B. was at the Lathlain Park game. He may never have returned to the group in 1986. Mike B. and I no longer saw each other daily at high school in 1986 as had been the case in 1984 and 1985. Without Mike the cheer squad would have been like the Clash in 1984-85 without Mick Jones (with just Joe Strummer and Paul Simonon remaining)!

I do recall sitting with my good mate Thommo behind the goals one day at Leederville Oval a few weeks after the Round 1 Perth match. I do not recall whether the cheer squad actually existed at this point. I think it probably did but in a smaller and less organized form. Thommo told me that he had left school and was doing a plastering subcontract job at the Parmelia Hotel. He would have been 16 by this time while I was 17 (see Appendix A). West Perth's declining performances in 1986 and the shadow of Western Australia's entry into the national competition dampened people's enthusiasm for the WAFL throughout 1986 and this affected people's moods certainly. It could be said that 1985 was the last year of the WAFL's Golden Era as by 1986 West Coast Eagles existed as a shadow in people's minds although not yet as an actual club with a name, jersey, and players (not until after the 1986 season had concluded).

The familiar world of government high-schools and junior football clubs produces the appearance of sameness and an egalitarian atmosphere which is often genuine but also, to some extent, does hide real economic and social divisions as well as just diverse interests. Each one of the group members of high-school age attended government high-schools (with the exception of Ben McA.) which are levelling environments. When I went to university in February 1986 it seemed to break the spell of sameness or maybe it just made me "feel different". I no longer saw Mike B. regularly in 1986 as high-school was over and Mike may well have not returned to the group at all in 1986. With both of the founders approaching or over 18-years-old the wider world was opening up and new interests and challenges were coming to the fore.

I do regret giving up on the cheer squad so easily and casually but we also must remember that the times were changing by 1986. The WAFL Commission was fast putting together a deal to join the expanded VFL competition above the heads of ordinary football supporters. This is not to imply that the majority of Western Australian football supporters did not in 1987 support the entry of West Coast Eagles into the expanded VFL but simply that ordinary football supporters were not directly consulted on the move through community consultation, public meetings, and / or some sort of voting process. Only in the year 2000 would the former East Fremantle and Swan Districts' player and Claremont and Fremantle Dockers' coach Gerard Neesham lead a resistance movement, Save West Australian Football Lobby or SWAFL, to try to re-claim the spirit of Western Australian football from the corporate people who had been first attracted to the game circa 1983-84. All of these negotiations and distractions affected adversely the mood at the grassroots and WAFL crowds did fall off significantly in 1986 (total qualifying round crowds 623,000 or 7,417 per game) although the drop was nowhere near as great as the 50% further drop-off in 1987 (total qualifying round crowds 308,000 or 3,667 per game), the first year post-Eagles. As a point of comparison, qualifying round crowds had been as high as 810,113 or 9,644 per game in 1970.

West Perth also performed disappointingly on the field in 1986, dropping out of the final-four whereas in 1985, under new coach John Wynne, the league-team had finished third at the end of the home-and-away rounds, and then played in and lost the first semi-final to give the team an eventual fourth position. All of these factors led to the cheer squad quietly disintegrating before the members' eyes in the first few home-and-away games of 1986. It is still hard to believe that it could just die off quietly without anyone consciously killing it. Mike B. and I had put in great efforts to organize the cheer squad for two years and to keep strong and healthy relationships alive within the group (which is not as easy as it may sound with the benefit of hindsight). When this combined effort was no longer applied, the foot was off the accelerator, and the cheer squad simply vanished. I have not seen any of the other members since 1986 (or perhaps 1987 or 1988), not even at West Perth games. Mike B. and I caught up on the Gold Coast in September 2009 and again in Kalgoorlie on 14 July 2011. A picture on the WAFL Golden Era website shows Mike B. (left) and me at the historic Exchange Hotel, Kalgoorlie, Western Australia on 14 July 2011. This picture was taken by a barmaid whom, appropriately enough given the themes in this book, was a West Ham United supporter.

South Fremantle's young talent outclasses a West Perth team caught like a deer in the headlights at Fremantle Oval

SOUTH FREMANTLE v WEST PERTH
ROUND 19 (9 AUGUST) 1986
I once talked to Pete C. and spent the game with him on the scoreboard bank's concrete terracing at Fremantle Oval (at around the half-forward flank position closest to the northern-end goals) for a match against South Fremantle late in the 1986 season. The flags had vanished and there was only the two of us left at this point in time. Pete C. and I hadn't even arranged in advance to meet; it was a chance meeting. I would have to say that the cheer squad no longer even existed by this time. However, Pete's charming, quiet, and thoughtful manner had not changed.

    After the game Pete C. and I walked through the Fremantle city streets together and I think Pete took a Number 106 bus or a train back to Perth while I took a different bus to Booragoon. We probably parted at Fremantle train station. I originally wrote this paragraph 26 years later, on 9 January 2013, and I still haven't seen Pete again since that day at Fremantle Oval near to the close of the 1986 season. As we walked through the Fremantle city streets together, as the dark and the chill started drifting in from the ocean (minimum temperatures were 4.5 and 4.0 degrees Celsius on Saturday 9th and Sunday 10th August 1986), we were both fairly subdued and disappointed as it looked like our team's season was over (the team probably could not make the final-four) and all the hope of the past two years had come to nothing. I think that another reason for my anxious and melancholic mood was the realization, pushed to the back of my mind, that my life was changing and it would never be the same again. I was 17-years-old, in the first year of university, and the adult world of responsibilities, choices, careers, and consequences was fast closing in, whilst childhood was at an end. In football terms, there was also massive change at work behind the scenes as the powerbrokers were putting together and planning for the new as yet unnamed super-team which would play in the VFL in 1987. Every genuine football person in Perth knew that the WAFL would never be the same again no matter how upbeat the newspapers were. Like my childhood, the old WAFL was slipping away. The days of fourteen thousand plus crowds at the match-of-the-round were never coming back.

The story of the West Perth Cheer Squad of 1984-86 draws to a close here. I will only add that I once saw the back of Mike C.'s head in the front section of a Number 103 bus which was heading from Perth to Fremantle later in 1986 (or possibly in 1987 or 1988) but I never had the chance to go and talk with him. I had got on the bus in Perth city-centre and had to exit at Nedlands to go to a lecture class at the University of Western Australia. I sometimes wish that I had stayed on the bus and gone to talk to Mike but I was the victim of a mind switched on only to daily routine and obligation. This encounter seemed somewhat symbolic of the separation which had developed between all the former mates once the cheer squad no longer existed. That was the last contact I had with any of them until meeting Mike B. by chance at a deli in Myaree in 1990 and then, 25 years later, catching up with him purposefully on the Gold Coast in September 2009 and again in Kalgoorlie on 14 July 2011. It is appropriate to end this chapter in a rather abrupt fashion, almost in the middle of a sentence or a train of thought, as that mirrors the actual ending of the West Perth Cheer Squad in 1986.

POSTSCRIPT

I close this book with reference to that ex-West Perth player of the 1980s, the Balga boy Dean Laidley. Laidley resigned as coach of AFL club North Melbourne on 16 June 2009 as, although he was a successful coach in the traditional mould, he could not or would not "sell" the club to sponsors as the new corporatized football world demanded. He is a figure of a bygone era and it is suitable to end this unashamedly traditionalist book with reference to him. Laidley is one important link between this chapter and the three which preceded it. A much younger Laidley was one of the players our cheer squad members watched and shouted for when he played for West Perth in 1984-85 and the Perth suburb of Balga also features significantly in this book. During 1984 or 1985, our friends from Chapters 3 to 5, P.A., Rex Tong, Thommo, and Robbie may well have encountered Laidley in

the run-down and depressing suburban shopping-centre in Balga or
at one of the suburb's service stations or at the famous Brian
Burke Reserve (home ground of the Balga Soccer Club whose heyday
was also in the 1980s).

By the late-2000s, the humble Laidley, who consistently
refused "corporate-speak" and always remained a Balga boy, was
no longer perceived by the powerful football elite to be in step
with the demands placed on senior team coaches by clubs and by
the AFL in this era of corporate football. Likewise, as a
traditionalist, I am pleased to say that I was there for the
last Golden Era of the WAFL. Football will literally never be
the same again.

This book is an attempt to preserve some of the memories,
from both sides of the boundary fence, and transmit them, if
only imperfectly, to the future generations who will be raised
knowing only West Coast, Fremantle, and the AFL. As a
traditional WAFL supporter, what can I say about West Coast? To
take the words of the club's song and cheekily alter its
meaning: "For years they took the best of us and claimed them
for their own". However, the similarity to the song ends there
because in this case "nobody is coming home" anymore from either
of the Perth-based AFL clubs to the WAFL (with the exception of
Peter Bell and a few other old diehards). Even John Worsfold and
Glen Jakovich, names revered in Perth up until today, didn't
bother turning out to play one final season with South Fremantle
as a way of saying thank-you to the original WAFL club which ten
years previously had been the springboard from which they
launched their VFL/AFL careers. To those football people who
continue to disrespect or ignore the traditional WAFL clubs and
their histories I will leave them with a biblical reference:
"give honour where honour is due". We should remember that our
ancestors going back 115 years loved these clubs and poured
their hearts and souls into them. Why should we forget them?

REFERENCES CONSULTED

Allan, J. (1989), Bloody Casuals: Diary of a Football Hooligan (Elton: Famedram Publishers).

Armstrong, G. (1998), Football Hooligans: Knowing the Score, paperback edition (Oxford: Berg).

Armstrong, G. and R. Harris (1991), "Football hooliganism: theory and evidence", Sociological Review, Vol. 39, No. 3, pp. 427-58.

Astrinakis, A. E. (2002), "Subcultures of hard-core fans in West Attica: an analysis of some central research findings", in Dunning, E., Murphy, P., Waddington, I. and Astrinakis, A. E. (Eds.), Fighting Fans: Football Hooliganism as a World Phenomenon (Dublin: University College Press).

Atkinson, B. A. (2008), It's a Grand Old Flag: a History and Comprehensive Statistical Analysis of the West Perth Football Club (Joondalup: West Perth Football Club).

Badiou, A. (2009), Theory of the Subject, Bosteels, B. (Trans.) (London and New York: Continuum).

Bairner, A. (2002), "The dog that didn't bark? Football hooliganism in Ireland", in Dunning, E., Murphy, P., Waddington, I. and Astrinakis, A. E. (Eds.), Fighting Fans: Football Hooliganism as a World Phenomenon (Dublin: University College Press).

Barker, A. J. (Tony) (2004), Behind the Play...a History of Football in Western Australia from 1868 (Perth: West Australian Football Commission).

Benigno, J. (2010), Rules for New York Sports Fans (Chicago: Triumph Books).

Bennett, J. G. (2009), E.1: a Journey through Whitechapel and Spitalfields (Nottingham: Five Leaves Publications).

Bestley, R. (2011), "From 'London's Burning' to 'Sten Guns in Sunderland'", Punk & Post-Punk, Vol. 1, No. 1, pp. 41-71.

Bosteels, B. (2010), "The leftist hypothesis: communism in the age of terror", in Douzinas, C. and Žižek, S. (Eds.), The Idea of Communism (London and New York: Verso).

Brabazon, T. (1998), "What's the story Morning Glory? Perth Glory and the imagining of Englishness", Sporting Traditions, Vol. 14, No. 2, pp. 53-66.

Brown, M. and B. Hansen (1994), Mal Brown & Mongrels I've Met (Mt Waverley: Brian Edward Hansen).

Byrne, L. (1984), "Protests hit Sandover 'muddle'", The West Australian, 29 August, p. 128.

Casey, K. (n/d but probably 1996), The Tigers' Tale: the Origins and the History of the Claremont Football Club (Perth: Kevin Casey).

Cherry, B. and M. Mellins (2011), "Negotiating the Punk in
    Steampunk: Subculture, Fashion & Performative Identity", Post
    & Post-Punk, Vol. 1, No. 1, pp. 5-25.
Chester, M. (2003), Naughty, paperback version (Wrea Green,
    Lancashire: Milo Books) [Stoke City hooligans].
Christian, G. (1984), "Three-way tie for the Sandover", The West
    Australian, 29 August, p. 127.
Christian, G. (1985a), "Swans prepare for an early blitz", The
    West Australian, 30 August, pp. 191-2.
Christian, G. (1985b), "Injuries sour West Perth's bid for
    glory", The West Australian, 26 August, p. 88.
Christian, G., Lee, J. and B. Messenger (1985), The Footballers:
    a History of Football in Western Australia (Perth: St George
    Books).
Cliff, T. (1996), "Trotsky on substitutionism", in Callinicos,
    A. (Ed.), Party and Class: Essays by Tony Cliff, Duncan
    Hallas, Chris Harman and Leon Trotsky, (London: Bookmarks).
Critchley, C. (2010), Our Footy: Real Fans vs Big Bucks
    (Melbourne: Wilkinson Publishing).
Dawson, B. (2004), John Todd: Six Decades of Footy (West
    Leederville: Cambridge Publishing).
Duke, V. and L. Crolley (1996), Football, Nationality and the
    State (London: Longman).
Duke, V. and P. Slepi?ka (2002), "Bohemian rhapsody: football
    supporters in the Czech Republic", in Dunning, E., Murphy,
    P., Waddington, I. and Astrinakis, A. E. (Eds.), Fighting
    Fans: Football Hooliganism as a World Phenomenon (Dublin:
    University College Press).
Dunning, E. (1994), "The social roots of football hooliganism: a
    reply to the critics of the 'Leicester School'" in
    Giulianotti, R., Bonney, M. and Hepworth, M. (Eds.), Football
    Violence and Social Identity (London and New York:
    Routledge), pp. 128-57.
Dunning, E. (1999), Sport Matters: Sociological Studies of
    Sport, Violence and Civilisation (London and New York:
    Routledge).
Dunning, E., Murphy, P. and I. Waddington (1991),
    "Anthropological versus sociological approaches to the study
    of football hooliganism: some critical notes", Sociological
    Review, Vol. 39, No. 3, pp. 459-78.
Dunning, E., Murphy, P. and I. Waddington (2002), "Towards a
    sociological understanding of football hooliganism as a world
    phenomenon", in Dunning, E., Murphy, P., Waddington, I. and
    Astrinakis, A. E. (Eds.), Fighting Fans: Football Hooliganism
    as a World Phenomenon (Dublin: University College Press), pp.
    1-22.

East, A. (2009), 75 Years of...Black & White, the Swan Districts
    Football Club (Perth: Swan Districts Football Club).
East, A., Kennedy, P., Lawrence, B. and J. Wicks (2005), From
    Redlegs to Demons: a History of the Perth Football Club from
    1899 (Perth: Perth Football Club).
Engels, F. (1968), "Preface to the Peasant War in Germany", in
    Karl Marx & Frederick Engels Selected Works (New York:
    International Publishers).
Engels, F. (2004), Socialism: Utopian and Scientific (New York:
    International Publishers).
Fevola, B. (2012), Fev: In my Own Words, with Adam McNicol,
    hardcover edition (Richmond: Hardie Grant Books).
Franklin, R. (2012), Fev Unauthorised: the Biography of Brendan
    Fevola, Football's Flawed Genius, paperback edition
    (Richmond: Slattery Media Group).
Frost, L. (2005), Immortals: Football People and the Evolution
    of Australian Rules (Melbourne: John Wiley & Sons).
Gardner, B. (2006), Good Afternoon Gentlemen, the Name's Bill
    Gardner, with C. Pennant (London: John Blake Publishing).
Giulianotti, R. (2002), "Supporters, Followers, Fans and
    Flaneurs: a Taxonomy of Spectator Identities in World
    Football", Journal of Sport and Social Issues, Vol. 26, No.
    1, pp. 25-46.
Giulianotti, R. and M. Gerrard (2001), "Cruel Brittania? Glasgow
    Rangers, Scotland and 'hot' football rivalries", in
    Armstrong, G. and Giulianotti, R. (Eds.), Fear and Loathing
    in World Football (Oxford and New York: Berg), pp. 23-42.
Giulianotti, R. and R. Robertson (2009), Globalization &
    Football, paperback edition (London: SAGE Publications).
Gorman, S. (2005), BrotherBoys: the Story of Jim and Phillip
    Krakouer (St. Leonard's: Allen & Unwin).
Harman, C. (1996), "Party and class", in Callinicos, A. (Ed.),
    Party and Class: Essays by Tony Cliff, Duncan Hallas, Chris
    Harman and Leon Trotsky (London: Bookmarks).
Hinde, S. and V. Mayberry (2011), "New Year's leave: Fev's
    career on knife's edge after latest drama", The Sunday Mail
    [Brisbane], 2 January, p. 3.
Hobbs, D. and D. Robins (1991), "The boy done good: football
    violence, changes and continuities", Sociological Review,
    Vol. 39, No. 3, pp. 551-9.
Hornby, N. (2009), Fever Pitch (Melbourne: Penguin Australia).
Hughson, J. (1997a), "Football, folk dancing and fascism:
    diversity and difference in multicultural Australia",
    Australian & New Zealand Journal of Sociology, Vol. 33, No.
    2, pp. 167-86.
Hughson, J. (1997b), "The Bad Blue Boys and the 'magical
    recovery' of John Clarke", in Armstrong, G. and Giulianotti,

R. (Eds.), Entering the Field: New Perspectives on World Football (London and New York: Berg), Chapter 12, pp. 239-59.

Hughson, J. (1999), "A tale of two tribes: expressive fandom in Australian soccer's A-league", Sport in Society, Vol. 2, No. 3, pp. 10-30.

Hughson, J. (2000), "The boys are back in town: soccer support and the social reproduction of masculinity", Journal of Sport and Social Issues, Vol. 24, No. 1, pp. 8-23.

Hughson, J. (2002), "Australian soccer's 'ethnic tribes': a new case for the carnivalesque", in Dunning, E., Murphy, P., Waddington, I. and Astrinakis, A. E. (Eds.), Fighting Fans: Football Hooliganism as a World Phenomenon (Dublin: University College Press).

Hunt, R. and G. Bond (2005), The Fat Lady sings: 40 Years in Footy (Southbank: News Custom Publishing).

James, K., Tolliday, C. and R. Walsh (2011), "Where to now, Melbourne Croatia?: Football Federation Australia's use of accounting numbers to institute exclusion upon ethnic clubs", Asian Review of Accounting, Vol. 19, No. 2, pp. 112-24.

James, K. and R. Walsh (2018), "The expropriation of goodwill and migrant labour in the transition to Australian football's A-League", International Journal of Sport Management and Marketing, Vol. 18, No. 5, pp. 430-52.

Johnstone, M. (2012), Saturday is Service Day, revised edition with new addendum (Motherwell: Motherwell Daft Productions) [Motherwell Saturday Service firm].

Lee, J. (1976), Old Easts: 1948-1975 (East Fremantle: East Fremantle Football Club).

Lydon, J., Zimmerman, K. and K. Zimmerman (1994), Rotten: No Irish, no Blacks, no Dogs (London: Plexus Publishing).

Lynch, R. L. and A. J. Veal (1996), Australian Leisure (South Melbourne: Longman).

Mao, Z. D. (1971), "On contradiction", in Selected Readings from the Works of Mao Tsetung (Beijing: Foreign Languages Press), Part IV, pp. 109-17.

Marsh, P. (1978), Aggro: the Illusion of Violence, hardcover edition (London: J M Dent & Sons).

Marx, K. H. (1968), "The Eighteen Brumaire of Louis Bonaparte", in Karl Marx & Frederick Engels Selected Works (New York: International Publishers).

Marx, K. H. (1976), Capital: A Critique of Political Economy Volume 1, Fowkes, B. (Trans.) (London: Penguin Classics), p. 1065.

Marx, K. H. (1977), A Contribution to the Critique of Political Economy, Preface (Moscow: Progress Publishers); available online:

http://www.marxists.org/archive/marx/works/1859/critique-pol-economy/preface.htm [accessed 23 August 2011].

Marx, K. H. and F. Engels (1968), "Manifesto of the Communist Party", in Karl Marx & Frederick Engels Selected Works (New York: International Publishers).

McColl, G. (2008), The Official Biography of Celtic: if you know the History (London: Headline Publishing).

Merleau-Ponty, M. (1969), Humanism and Terror (Boston: Beacon Press).

Morris, D (1978), "Foreword", in Marsh, P., Aggro: the Illusion of Violence, hardcover edition (London: J M Dent & Sons), p. 7.

Muyt, A. (2006), Maroon and Blue: Recollections and Tales of the Fitzroy Football Club (Carlton North: The Vulgar Press).

Nimac, I., Duševi?, Š., Lozina, L. and T. Nimac (2008), More than the Game: 50 Years of Sydney United (Edensor Park: Sydney United Football Club).

O'Kane, J. (2006), Celtic Soccer Crew: what the hell do we care? (London: Pennant Books).

Panfichi, A. and J. Thieroldt (2002), "Barras Bravas: representation and crowd violence in Peruvian football", in Dunning, E., Murphy, P., Waddington, I. and Astrinakis, A. E. (Eds.), Fighting Fans: Football Hooliganism as a World Phenomenon (Dublin: University College Press).

Pennant, C. (2003), Congratulations, you have just met the I.C.F. (West Ham United) (London: John Blake Publishing).

Pennant, C. (2008), Cass (London: John Blake Publishing).

Pennant, C. and R. Silvester (2004), Rolling with the 6.57 Crew: the True Story of Pompey's Legendary Football Fans, paperback edition (London: John Blake Publishing).

Pennant, C. and M. Smith (2007), Want Some Aggro? The True Story of West Ham's First Guv'nors, paperback edition (London: John Blake Publishing).

Rousseau, J.-J. (1968), The Social Contract (London: Penguin Classics).

Roversi, A. and Balestri, C. (2002), "Italian ultras today: change or decline?" in Dunning, E., Murphy, P., Waddington, I. and Astrinakis, A. E. (Eds.), Fighting Fans: Football Hooliganism as a World Phenomenon (Dublin: University College Press), pp. 131-42.

Sandercock, L. and I. Turner (1981), Up Where, Cazaly? The Great Australian Game (Sydney: Granada).

Scott, C. (2005), Will the Real Mary Kelly...? (London: Christopher Scott).

Slaughter, P. (1975), Marxism & the Class Struggle (London: New Park Publications), Chapter VII; available online:

http://www.marxists.org/reference/subject/philosophy/works/en
/slaughte.htm [accessed 23 August 2011].

Souvarine, B. (1939), Stalin: a Critical Survey of Bolshevism,
James, C. L. R. (Trans.) (London: Alliance Book Corp.
Longman, Green and Co.), Chapter VIII; available online:
http://www.marxists.org/history/etol/writers/souvar/works/sta
lin/ch08.htm [accessed 23 August 2011].

Stalin, J. V. (1976), "The results of the first five-year plan:
Report delivered at the Joint Plenum of the Central Committee
and the Central Control Commission
of the C.P.S.U.(B.) January 7, 1933", in Problems of Leninism
(Beijing: Foreign Languages Press), pp. 578-630; available
online: http://www.marx2mao.com/Stalin/RFFYP33.html [accessed
23 August 2011].

Stocks, G. (1985a), "Disappointing end for Kim Rogers", The West
Australian, 2 September, p. 72.

Stocks, G. (1985b), "A driving force ...", The West Australian,
31 August, p. 192.

Stocks, G. (1986), "Smith gives Demons more grit", The West
Australian, 31 March, p. 68.

Stocks, G. (1987), "West Perth pace key factor", The West
Australian, 28 March, p. 200.

Vattimo, G. (2010), "Weak communism?" in Douzinas, C. and Žižek,
S. (Eds.), The Idea of Communism (London and New York:
Verso), pp. 205-7.

Warren, J. (2003), Sheilas, Wogs and Poofters: an Incomplete
Biography of Johnny Warren and Soccer in Australia, with A.
Harper and J. Whittington (North Sydney: Random House).

Young, K. (2002), "A walk on the wild side: exposing North
American sports crowd disorder", in Dunning, E., Murphy, P.,
Waddington, I. and Astrinakis, A. E. (Eds.), Fighting Fans:
Football Hooliganism as a World Phenomenon (Dublin:
University College Press), pp. 201-17.

APPENDIX A - Sub-gangs, West Perth Cheer Squad, 1984-86 (ages as at 1984)

The Booragoon sub-gang

1 *Kevin J. (name changed), 15 years, Applecross Senior High School student (1984-85) then university student (1986)

2 *Mike B., 16 years, Applecross Senior High School (1984-85) then occupation unknown (1986), school friend of Kevin.

The Carine sub-gang

3 Courtney, 14 years, high-school student, junior football friend of Thommo

4 Rohan H., 14 years, high-school student, school friend of Courtney

Floaters / non-aligned

5 *Mark T. aka "Thommo", 14 years, high-school student (1984-85), plasterer (1986); junior football friend of Courtney

6 *Robbie, 14 years, joined cheer squad 1985, lived in Balga, took buses home with Balga sub-gang, knew Thommo before joining cheer squad, also in Balga sub-gang

The Balga sub-gang

7 *"P.A.", 18 years, lived in Balga, employment situation unknown

8 *Rex Tong (name changed), 16 years, lived in nearby Tuart Hill but took buses to games with P.A. and Robbie, school / employment situation unknown

The C. brothers sub-gang

9 *Mike C., 16 years, in and out of reform homes

10 *Robert C., 15 years, only went to games occasionally, had criminal record

11 *Pete C., 14 years, in and out of reform homes

12 *Female niece or cousin of the C. brothers, 4 years, attended 50% of games

The Perth Modern SHS sub-gang

13 Ben McA., 13-14 years, John XIII college student

14 Rob, 13-14 years old, Perth Modern SHS student, friend of Ben and Tony

15 Tony, 12-13 years, Perth Modern SHS student, school friend of Rob

16 Mario, 8-9 years, younger brother of Tony (also in younger members sub-gang)

The younger members sub-gang

17 Michael aka "Half", 8 years, parents were financial members of West Perth, no relationship to other cheer squad members, lived in Bayswater or Maylands

18 *"Thommo Junior", 8 years, younger brother of Thommo

(* denotes took public transport to and from games)

APPENDIX B – Selected West Perth match results, 1976-86
Round 6, 1984 – West Perth v South Fremantle, Leederville Oval
Likely line-ups
(Source: The West Australian, Saturday, 5 May, 1984, p. 193)
West Perth FC
Backs: Dayman, Comerford, O'Brien
Half-backs: Hendriks, Mugavin, Morgan
Centres: Warwick, Perrin, Mifka
Half-forwards: Simms, Lockman, Gastevich
Forwards: Bell, Alderton, Bogunovich
Ruck: Nelson, Menaglio, Fong
Interchange from: Kickett, Michalczyk, Davis, D Falconer
South Fremantle FC
Backs: Barrett, Hayes, G Carter
Half-backs: Mosconi, Henworth, Cornell
Centres: Keyner, Hardie, Grljusich
Half-forwards: Michael, Dorotich, Vigona
Forwards: Matera, Mount, N Carter
Ruck: Edwards, Vasoli, Hart
Interchange from: Rawlinson, Gillica, Winmar, Amoroso

Match results
West Perth FC 3.5 6.811.15 15.15 (105) drew South Fremantle FC
3.4 8.7 9.7 16.7 (105)
Scorers: WP: Kickett 4.1, Davis 3.0, Gastevich 2.1, Simms 1.4,
Lockman, Menaglio, Nelson 1.1, Fong, Perrin 1.0, Mifka 0.3,
Michalczyk 0.1, Warwick 0.1, Forced 0.1.
SF: Hart 4.0, Winmar 3.1, Hardie, Matera 2.1, Dorotich 2.0,
Edwards 1.3, Hayes 1.1, Vasoli 1.0, N Carter 0.1, Forced 0.1.
Best-on-ground rankings: B Perrin (WP) 1, W Mosconi (SF) 2, G
Michalczyk (WP) 3.
Team rankings
WP: B Perrin 1, G Michalczyk 2, D Warwick 3, J Gastevich 4, P
Mifka 5, D Kickett 6.
SF: W Mosconi 1, D Hart 2, B Hardie 3, W Matera 4, R Barrett 5,
P Vasoli 6.
B Perrin: "Gave a brilliant ruck-roving performance. Had 18
kicks, took six marks and made nine handpasses".
W Mosconi: "Improved as the game progressed. Started on the
half-back line, but played mainly on the ball and on a wing".
G Michalczyk: "In his first league match for five weeks,
dominated the centre".
(Source: The West Australian, Monday, 7 May, 1984, p. 81)

Match analysis

Quotes from DAVD MARSH:

"One of the first decisions made by Dennis Cometti after his appointment as West Perth's coach before the 1982 season was to promote West Australian junior players.

"This is paying dividends, as evident when five first-year men played leading roles in helping West Perth to rise from almost certain defeat.

(The five first-year players were: Derek Kickett from Tammin; John Morgan from Merredin; local juniors Ron Davis and Paul Mifka; and Brendon Bell from Karratha.)

Ron Davis "played superbly to kick the last two goals of the game from difficult angles in a forward pocket".

Brian Perrin is "one of the few Victorian players to excel in WA football in recent years.

"The former Footscray player [Perrin] gave a brilliant ruck-roving performance to continually set up attacking moves through sheer hard work.

"Stephen Michael [SF] played steadily without having a major influence on the game".

(Source: David Marsh (1984), "Cometti's plan is paying off", The West Australian, Monday, 7 May, p. 80)

Round 16, 1984 – East Perth v West Perth, Perth Oval
This was the second close and exciting finish to West Perth versus East Perth "Perth derbies" during the 1984 home-and-away season. It is often said that Fremantle derbies are usually tough contests regardless of the positions of the two teams on the league ladder. The same could be said for Perth derbies. However, East Perth was in a rebuilding stage in 1984, like South Fremantle, and it only just made the finals series. Although West Perth was in the final-four after the loss in this Round 16 clash it finished the season badly and failed to make the finals. Following West Perth in the 1980s was a disheartening experience as the club often defeated leading teams only to lose games it should have won. In this game Les Fong and Peter Menaglio, as usual, were outstanding for West Perth. Both should be regarded as legendary names across the WAFL today but sadly that does not appear to be the case. Why not a "Les Fong-Robert Wiley" trophy for Perth versus West Perth games? It might make more sense than Stephen Michael-Barry Cable Cup (for Perth versus South Fremantle games) as at least Wiley and Fong actually played against each other and played the same position!

We note in this game West Perth coach Dennis Cometti again playing players out of position. Phil Bradmore was named at centre-half-back rather than in his customary centre-half-forward position while David Marsh's match report suggests the workmanlike but hardly charismatic ex-Swan Districts defender Graeme Comerford played at centre-half-forward! Craig Nelson was named at centre-half-forward rather than in the ruck. The 1983 Sandover Medallist John Ironmonger remained with East Perth in 1984 and he dominated West Perth's inexperienced ruckmen Stuart Crole and Ramsay Bogunovich. Craig Nelson does not appear to have played in the ruck although he was in the starting side according to Saturday's West Australian. The surprise success of country recruit Kim Rogers in the ruck for West Perth in 1985 is one factor which contributed to the club's finals appearance that year.

However, in this 1984 game, it was the type of game West Perth really should have won if it wanted to play finals football. East Perth was in the rebuilding stage but the club mixed new players with the remains of the 1978 premiership side very well and the club was very competitive in 1984 and never disgraced. In this East Perth team old-hands such as Grant Campbell, Stan Magro, Peter Spencer, and Wayne Otway (the only remaining 1978 premiership player in the team that day) played alongside many exciting young players who would go on to have great careers in the VFL/AFL including Glenn Bartlett, Michael Christian, Richard Dennis (out injured for this game), and the one and only Alex Ishchenko.

The 1984 WAFL season was extremely tightly fought, few teams were uncompetitive, and few teams were far ahead of the pack. Only ten premiership points separated South Fremantle (second) from Claremont (seventh). Leader East Fremantle could hardly have claimed to have dominated the season with 11 wins and 5 losses and a percentage of 110.31% after Round 16. Only one club, South Fremantle, had a percentage exceeding 120% and only last-placed Perth had a percentage below 85% (but a still very respectable 82.16%). Claremont (seventh) had won 7 and lost 9. Even the struggling Demons had won 4 games by Round 16. It is to the credit of past and present WAFL administrators and club leaders that the competition was so evenly poised and it suggests the zoning system was working well at this point. The competition had eight strong, traditional, and well-supported clubs all playing out of their traditional home grounds. This is very unlike the present AFL where of the Victorian clubs only Geelong, Melbourne, and arguably Richmond still plays matches at the traditional home ground.

My 1984 season notes, written during the 1984 season, state:

"East Perth 19.15 d West Perth 18.17. Perth Oval. Michael [Blewett] lost lens at Claisebrook Station. Huge record cheer squad – talked to [West Perth coach Dennis] Cometti before the match. Timeclock wasn't working – thrilling last quarter. Great games by [John] Gastev and [Derek] Kickett" [underlining in original].

There was a large group of people in the West Perth Cheer Squad that day. It was a fine day and the team was playing the traditional rivals. I think that the cheer squad had its complete contingent of around 15 dedicated members there that day, plus the many hangers-on you would get at away games. It was a happy carnival-like atmosphere as most away games for the group were. Dennis Cometti talked to the group members from across the fence before the match. The group probably had around 10 to 15 red-and-blue flags. It was a "thrilling last quarter", I wrote in 1984, and the time clock was not working at this stage of the match. I listed John Gastev and Derek Kickett as West Perth's best two players while David Marsh of The West Australian listed these two as third and fourth best respectively. The West Perth cheer squad members enjoyed the thrilling finish and we were not too distressed to lose the game. A large cheer squad group walked back through the old entrance (now gone) at the south-east corner of the ground and headed back to Claisebrook Station. My season notes record that the joint founder Mike B. lost his contact lens at Claisebrook Station after the match. Group members took a long time looking for it.

The whole group took up nearly one carriage on the city-bound train. At Perth station group members split up and the majority of the members went to take their various buses back to the northern suburbs. (This was before the building of the Clarkson train line.) Mike B. and I headed through the city streets to St George's Terrace to take the Number 105 bus to Booragoon, still holding one giant red-and-blue flag each. Mike and I often met the Perth and Claremont cheer squads in the city-centre in those days and everyone from all groups would exchange friendly greetings and match results much like the Victorian cheer squads of that era used to do at Flinders Street Station. This day in 1984 was a fantastic match in the best tradition of the WAFL Golden Era, played between two traditional rivals with a good atmosphere and on a lovely fine day. Our cheer squad then was one of the largest groups we ever managed to assemble. This day was probably the first when the cheer squad existed in mature form and it was one of its best days. I remember a great atmosphere of camaraderie among the group increased by Dennis Cometti exchanging a conversation with group members before the game. The large Aboriginal pro-East Perth family groups that used to sit under the big trees behind the southern-end goals gave the cheer squad absolutely no problems nor we them. Bassendean Oval in 1985 would not be quite so welcoming.

Likely line-ups:
(Source: The West Australian, Saturday, 21 July, 1984, p. 189)
East Perth FC
Backs: Magro, Kohlmann, Christian
Half-backs: Fullarton, Bartlett, Sheldon
Centres: Carpenter, Blakely, Solin
Half-forwards: R Sparks, Campbell, D Morgan
Forwards: Ironmonger, Scott, Papotto
Rucks: Ishchenko, Spencer, Otway
Interchange: Cocker, Walsh
In: R Sparks, Ishchenko, Magro, Walsh
Out: K Sparks, Berry, Kavanagh, Dennis (ankle)

West Perth FC
Backs: Dayman, Hendriks, Comerford
Half-backs: O'Brien, Bradmore, J Morgan
Centres: Warwick, Michalczyk, Mifka
Half-forwards: D Kickett, Nelson, Gastev
Forwards: Bogunovich, Simms, Davis
Ruck: Crole, Menaglio, Fong
Interchange: Bell, Mountain

Selections:
KEN CASELLAS: East Perth
DAVID MARSH: West Perth
GARY STOCKS: West Perth
ROBERT WAINWRIGHT: West Perth
TIM GOSSAGE: East Perth
(Source: The West Australian, Saturday, 21 July, 1984, p. 189)

Match results — Saturday 21 July, 1984, Perth Oval
East Perth FC 2.5 9.9 14.12 19.15 (129) d West Perth FC 1.5 7.9
12.12 18.17 (125)
Scorers: EP: R Sparks 4.2, Papotto 3.3, Campbell 3.0, Otway 2.1,
Solin 2.0, Scott 1.4, Spencer 1.2, Blakely 1.1, Carpenter 1.0,
Ironmonger 1.0, Morgan 0.1, Fullarton 0.1.
WP: D Simms 5.1, Kickett 4.3, Gastev 3.2, Fong 2.0, Hendriks
1.1, Nelson 1.1, Bradmore 1.1, Warwick 1.0, Menaglio 0.3,
Comerford 0.3, Mifka 0.1, Forced 0.1.
Weather: Fine, moderate southerly breeze.
(Source: The West Australian, Monday, 23 July, 1984, p. 85)
Attendance: 8,505 (from WAFL Online)
Free kicks: EP: 9, 8, 5, 5 — 27.
WP: 11, 9, 11, 4 — 35.
(Source: The West Australian, Monday, 23 July, 1984, p. 85)

Best players:
1 John Ironmonger (EP) — Was a dominant ruckman throughout.
Knocked the ball intelligently, marked strongly and used
constructive handball.
2 Peter Menaglio (WP) — A strong and creative ruck-roving
performance, with a particularly brilliant second half.
3 Russell Sparks (EP) — An enterprising performance on a half-
forward flank where he continually set up attacking moves.
Team rankings:
EP: J Ironmonger 1, R Sparks 2, G Campbell 3, W Otway 4, M
Blakely 5, D Morgan 6.
WP: P Menaglio 1, L Fong 2, J Gastev 3, D Kickett 4, P Bradmore
5, D Warwick 6.

(Source: The West Australian, Monday, 23 July, 1984, p. 85)

Match analysis:
Quotes from DAVID MARSH:
"East Perth's rush towards the 1984 final round [PB note: echoes of 1978] gained momentum at Perth Oval on Saturday when they forced West Perth to stagger and then fall at the end of a contest that was survival of the fittest.
"East Perth, 10 points down late in the final quarter, recovered to win by four points – 19.15 to 18.17.
"It was a magnificent game in which the East Perth players, after appearing on the brink of being over-run by West Perth, showed tremendous character to fight back and snatch this thrilling victory.
"However, West Perth's bid for success showed plenty of raw courage from a team which finished with only 15 fit men.
"West Perth lost veteran centreman George Michalczyk at the 12-minute mark of the first quarter with a dislocated shoulder, ruckman Ramsay Bogunovich at the six-minute mark of the second quarter with a knee injury, and centre-half-forward Graeme Comerford (elbow), full-back Geoff Hendriks (knee) and back-pocket player Wayne Dayman (ankle) [REST IN PEACE – the author] all carried injuries at the finish.
"Another shadow is over the club with brilliant half-forward Derek Kickett, Brian Perrin and John Morgan facing the tribunal tonight after being reported following separate incidents.
"It was not a happy day for West Perth. It was hard for them to accept the philosophy that the East Perth victory was what football needed to sustain more interest in which clubs will play in the 1984 final round.
"East Perth led 14.12 to 12.12 at three-quarter time, which stemmed from excellent ruck work from John Ironmonger, livewire roving from Wayne Otway and a dominant half-forward line of Russell Sparks, Grant Campbell and David Morgan.
"Strongly built Mark Blakely worked hard in the centre to instigate several forward thrusts for the home side and ruck-rover Peter Spencer played well in patches.
"West Perth's two best players were ruck-rover Peter Menaglio and rover Les Fong, who covered tremendous ground and were chief kick-getters.
"Fong finished the game with 27 kicks and Menaglio had 22 (with 14 in the second half). They provided West Perth with momentum on the ball and to a certain extent helped to nullify Ironmonger's dominance in the ruck.
"West Perth's half-forward flankers John Gastev and [Derek] Kickett were outstanding.

"Dean Warwick and Paul Mifka showed pace on the wings and Doug
Simms kicked West Perth's first four and their sixth goals from
full-forward".
(Source: David Marsh (1984), "East Perth's rush picks up", The
West Australian, Monday, 23 July, 1984, p. 84)

1985 First Semi-final – Swan Districts v West Perth, Subiaco Oval

Likely line-ups

(Source: The West Australian, Saturday, 31 August, 1985, p. 191)

West Perth FC

Backs: Munns, Comerford, Evans

Half-backs: Warwick, C Nelson, Mugavin

Centres: Mifka, Bell, D Bewick

Half-forwards: Murnane. Bradmore, Fong

Forwards: Chaplin, Stephens, Kickett

Ruck: Rogers, Laidley, C Bewick

Interchange: Gastev, A Nelson, N Fong, Turley

Swan Districts FC

Backs: Hetherington, Mullooly, Ware

Half-backs: Fogarty, Sartori, Skwirowski

Centres: Allen, Solin, Penny

Half-forwards: Hutton, Rance, Holmes

Forwards: Caton, Sidebottom, Kimberley

Ruck: Johns, Langsford, Taylor

Interchange: Ahmat, Holtzman, Outridge, Richardson, Maher

Selections:

GEOFF CHRISTIAN: Swan Districts

KEN CASELLAS: West Perth

DAVID MARSH: Swan Districts

GARY STOCKS: West Perth

TIM GOSSAGE: West Perth

MAL BROWN (PERTH COACH): Swan Districts

GRAHAM MOSS (CLAREMONT COACH): West Perth

Rival coaches' predictions:

MAL BROWN (PERTH COACH): "West Perth's biggest asset is their pace and Peter Menaglio will be a loss in that regard. In addition, Peter Murnane and George Michalczyk are under an injury cloud and that could see them struggle to maintain pressure midfield.

"If West Perth had all their little men fit I think they would win. But Swan Districts get players like Jon Fogarty, Kevin Taylor, Tom Mullooly and Joe Ahmat back for this game and that must give them a boost.

"On the other hand, West Perth have a lot of young players who will be playing in their first final. I think that who ever wins the game will play in the grand final".

GRAHAM MOSS (CLAREMONT COACH): "Swans have lost that bit of toughness which helped them cut out running players in recent years and I think they will have problems curbing the West Perth midfield players.

"Phil Bradmore has been in exceptional form at centre-half-forward and he complements the work of the smaller players.

"If West Perth have any problems they appear to be in defence where they will have to check players like Garry Sidebottom, Murray Rance and Brett Hutton [i.e. Brent Hutton].

"It will be important for Graeme Comerford and company to bring the ball to the ground and allow some of the smaller players to clear it.

"On their day West Perth are a very good side and if they get their tails up early they will be hard to beat. But I do not think they are as good as Subiaco or East Fremantle".
(Source: The West Australian, Saturday, 31 August, 1985, p. 191)

Match results
Swan Districts FC 7.3 12.6 17.8 24.14 (158) d West Perth FC 4.3 9.7 14.8 19.12 (126)
Scorers: SD: Sidebottom 9.1, Taylor 5.2, Holmes 5.1, Caton 3.1, Allen 1.1, Rance 1.0, Langsford 0.2, Ahmat, Hetherington, Ware, Solin 0.1, Forced 0.2.
WP: Bradmore 4.1, Kickett 4.1, D Bewick 3.1, C Bewick, Fong 2.2, Murnane 2.0, Chaplin 1.0, Gastev 1.0, Mifka, E vans, Munns 0.1, Forced 0.2.
Official attendance: 26,508 (from WAFL Online).
Weather: Fine.

Team rankings GEOFF CHRISTIAN:
SD: G Sidebottom 1, W Skwirowski 2, B Kimberley 3, M Johns 4, K Taylor 5, A Solin 6.
WP: P Bradmore 1, R Munns 2, D Bewick 3, P Mifka 4, B Bell 5, C Bewick 6.
KEN CASELLAS
SD: M Johns 1, G Sidebottom 2, K Taylor 3, A Solin 4, D Holmes 5, W Skwirowski 6.
WP: P Bradmore 1, C Bewick 2, D Bewick 3, R Munns 4, P Mifka 5, D Laidley 6.
DAVID MARSH
SD: G Sidebottom 1, B Kimberley 2, K Taylor 3, W Skwirowski 4, A Solin 5, M Johns 6.
WP: P Bradmore 1, R Munns 2, D Bewick 3, P Mifka 4, B Bell 5, C Bewick 6.
GARY STOCKS

SD: G Sidebottom 1, B Kimberley 2, W Skwirowski 3, A Solin 4, D
Holmes 5, M Johns 6
WP: P Bradmore 1, D Bewick 2, R Munns 3, P Mifka 4, C Bewick 5,
B Bell 6.
(Source: The West Australian, Monday 2 September, 1985, p. 73)

Selected match statistics (The West Australian, Monday 2
September, 1985, p. 73):
SD: G Sidebottom 5 marks-14 kicks-2 effective handballs; A Solin
3-18-12; B Kimberley 5-19-9; K Taylor 3-15-11.
WP: P Bradmore 8-18-3; C Bewick 3-20-4; D Bewick 2-19-4; R Munns
8-16-12; P Mifka 6-17-5; K Rogers 1-0-2; L Fong 8-16-8; J Gastev
7-13-4; P Murnane 4-9-2; D Laidley 2-15-2.

Coach's Comment:
John Wynne (WP): "I don't think you can be pleased with a losing
effort, but it does hold us in good stead for next year".
(Source: Gary Stocks (1985), "Disappointing end for Kim Rogers",
The West Australian, Monday, 2 September, p. 72)
Garry Sidebottom Comment: "Kicking goals is my business, so when
our other players work like they did today, it makes my job
easier"
(Source: David Marsh (1985), "Sidey's personal goal", The West
Australian, Monday, 2 September, p. 73)

Media quotes re Phil Bradmore's performance: "In Saturday's
match against Swan Districts, Bradmore capped off his most
successful season in league football with another outstanding
performance at centre-half-forward.
"He almost single-handedly kept the Falcons in the game in the
first three quarters and he finished with eight marks, 18 kicks
and three effective handpasses – and a suspected broken hand".
Bradmore's game was the "best performance of his career".
Bradmore "has developed into one of the game's most colourful
characters."
(Source: Gary Stocks (1985), "Bradmore proves his point", The
West Australian, Monday, 2 September, p. 72)

Match analysis
Quotes from the late GEOFF CHRISTIAN:
"The performances in all three grades have left West Perth with
a strong foundation from which to build their 1986 campaign.
"...it was to West Perth's credit that they managed 19.12 and
retained a chance of winning until early in the final quarter.
"The performance was a testimony to the Falcons' spirit of 1985.

"Bradmore received a meagre tally of 14 [Sandover] medal votes,
a classic case of where the work done by a player during a
season was undervalued.
"West Perth held an edge across the centreline.
Bradmore was "the best man afield" in the opinion of some.
"[Darren] Bewick confirmed that he is one of the game's most
exciting first year players.
Ross Munns was the "least experienced defender" but "most
effective".
"Full-back [Graeme] Comerford battled gamely against the in-form
Sidebottom who could do little, if anything wrong. In that mood
Sidebottom would kick goals, no matter [who] the opponent [was].
(Source: Geoff Christian (1985), "Falcons are on the right
track", The West Australian, Monday, 2 September, p. 72)

Round 1, 1986 - Perth v West Perth, Lathlain Park
Match results
Perth FC 6.3 10.8 11.10 13.15 (93) drew West Perth FC 1.2 6.7
9.11 13.15 (93)
Scorers: P: Rea 5.7, Wiley 3.0, Ryder 2.4, Cousins, Spalding,
Santostefano 1.0, Stasinowsky, Zaikos 0.1, Forced 0.2.
WP: D Bewick 3.4, Bradmore 3.2, Michalczyk 1.2, C Bewick, Fong,
Kickett, Evans 1.1, Stockley, Warwick 1.0, Menaglio, Mifka, King
0.1.
Official attendance: 8,121 (from WAFL Online).
Weather: Fine.

Best-on-ground rankings FOOTBALLER OF THE YEAR AWARD
P Menaglio (WP) 5 votes, D Laidley (WP) 4 votes, R Wiley (P) 3
votes, M Rea (P) 2 votes, C Smith (P) 1 vote.
Team rankings
P: R Wiley 1, M Rea 2, C Smith 3, M Watson 4, M Higgins 5, J
Lucas 6.
WP: P Menaglio 1, D Laidley 2, P Bradmore 3, K Rogers 4, L Fong
5, G Michalczyk 6.
P Menaglio: "An outstanding display in the uncustomary role of
half-back".
D Laidley: "Combined with Menaglio on the half-back line to
thwart many Perth attacking moves".
R Wiley: "A hard-working display and was at his best when Perth
needed him to claw their way back into the match".
M Rea: "Gave Perth an early lead with a brilliant first-half
five-goal haul".
C Smith: "Given the difficult assignment of checking live-wire
West Perth half-forward Derek Kickett and he did the job
admirably".
(Source: The West Australian, Monday, 31 March 1986, p. 68)

Match analysis:
Quotes from GARY STOCKS:
"It became obvious on Saturday that Perth have improved this
season.
"There is more depth to the club than there has been since 1978
when the Demons lost the grand final to East Perth.
Perth "unlucky not to win", "opened in brilliant style" with
Mick Rea "in superb touch at full-forward". Wiley "asserted
control midfield" in the first quarter. At the same time Jack
Lucas "eliminated" WP centreman Darren Bewick.
"West Perth are widely regarded as league football's most
skilful team...

West Perth "force[d] their way into the match" through half-backs Laidley and Menaglio, captain Fong, ruck-rover Michalczyk, and centre-half-forward Bradmore.
"A pleasing aspect from Perth's point of view was that they did not surrender when West Perth hit the front for the first time in the match at the 15-minutre mark of the last quarter".
(Source: Gary Stocks (1986), "Smith gives Demons more grit", The West Australian, Monday, 31 March, p. 68)

Round 19, 1986 – South Fremantle v West Perth, Fremantle Oval
This Round 19 match at Fremantle Oval was a match West Perth
really had to win to secure a final-four position, as David
Marsh wrote in his match preview in The West Australian on the
morning of the game (see below for the full-text of Marsh's
match preview). On paper it did not look a difficult proposition
for West Perth to win as the club was sitting on 8 wins, 9
losses, and a draw, with percentage of 89%, compared to South
Fremantle's 5 wins, 13 losses, and 72%. If West Perth could not
win a game against a rival with such a track record then
obviously it had little hope of ending the year successfully
even if it did scrape into the final-four. South Fremantle was
in a rebuilding year with the few older players still hanging
around from the premiership year of 1980, such as Benny Vigona,
entering their twilight years.

One interesting development of the last two years of the
WAFL prior to introduction of West Coast Eagles was the
surprising resurgence of depleted East Perth and South Fremantle
sides which were then, by necessity as much as by choice,
filling their senior teams with promising youngsters. These
young players had not yet begun to make a huge impression on the
scoreboard with these two clubs finishing sixth and seventh in
1986. However, both clubs contained large numbers of promising
juniors who would go on to forge successful VFL/AFL careers.
This shows the magnificent ability of the WAFL clubs, even at
this late stage of the game (one year prior to formation of West
Coast), to re-create themselves successfully from within during
down years by turning to talented juniors from the country and
metropolitan zones. A read through the selected teams of both
East Perth and South Fremantle in 1986 shows what great talents
were emerging. As David Marsh wrote, SFFC had begun the season
extremely poorly but slowly the young team had begun to gel and
pick up its self-confidence, playing with the enthusiasm of
youth mixed with that indomitable bulldog spirit. Marsh wrote
that South Fremantle had inflicted surprise mid-season defeats
upon the eventual premier Subiaco and the eventual third-placed
team Perth. South had won 2 and lost 3 since Round 13. Another
factor counting against West Perth this day was its bad record
at Fremantle Oval, traditionally a graveyard for WPFC teams.
Marsh wrote that the Falcons had not won at this windswept
ground in eight years prior to this match. This means that even
in 1982 when West Perth had finished third and in 1985 when West
Perth had finished fourth it had been unable to win against
South at South's home ground. Because of these factors, West
Perth fans who headed to Fremantle Oval this day in 1986 found
it hard to push aside feelings of dread and foreboding.

If we look at South Fremantle's nominated team, we can see it included a number of brilliant young players who would go on to achieve great success in the VFL/AFL. Starting from the back line and working forward, this included Peter Sumich at centre-half-back (a first-year player); Mark Bairstow in the centre (a second-year player); Neil "Nicky" Winmar on the half-forward flank (a fourth-year player); John Worsfold as ruck-rover (a first-year player); and Wally Matera as first rover (a fifth-year player). Other players who would not play VFL/AFL but who had great years at Fremantle Oval included Brad Collard on the left wing (a third-year player); Matt Sambrailo at full-forward (a first-year player); Derek Collard in the forward pocket / second rover (a second-year player); and the 1989 Sandover Medallist Craig Edwards as first ruckman (a third-year player). This would have been the beginnings of a new dynasty for South Fremantle had the VFL/AFL not intervened and picked all the best talent out of the side.

By contrast, the West Perth team was largely unchanged from the previous year but just a little older. It had some juniors coming through but not in the same numbers and not with the same quality as those at the port club. West Perth's best young players included John Gastev, Sean King, Dean Laidley, Paul Mifka, and Craig Turley, all of whom later played for West Coast. Another promising young player was Darren Bewick, probably the best of the lot, but his great success at Essendon probably surprised many who had watched him play in the WAFL. His elder brother Corry returned to West Perth in 1986 and he was one of the best and most consistent players for the club that year. Claremont player Simon Lill was really the only recruit of note to come from another WAFL club in 1986. The East Fremantle premiership player Gavin Wake was a sensational recruit for West Perth in 1987 but his impact was lost in the year when most football fans had turned their attentions from the WAFL to West Coast Eagles. If Wake had come over a year earlier it might have made a big difference as that type of toughness is hard to come by at West Perth (except for ruckmen) and has always had to be imported.

Like the 1985 first semi-final (West Perth versus Swan Districts) this was a demoralizing game to watch for WPFC fans as the result was never in doubt and the club was just overshadowed and outplayed in pretty much all positions without being completely disgraced. West Perth trailed 21.12 to 10.9 at three-quarter time and the game was obviously completely over. I remember sitting and watching this game with my friend 16-year-old Pete C. on the concrete terraces on the scoreboard wing at around the half-forward flank position at the city-end of the ground. Pete C. and I were the only remnants remaining of the

West Perth Cheer Squad which had sat behind the northern-end
goals at Leederville Oval during 1984-85. The group had
gradually disintegrated from its peak of 15-20 regulars starting
in Round 2 of the 1986 season as people just naturally drifted
apart due to life changes and with no-one making the mental
effort anymore to keep the group together. I only met Pete by
chance this day. Both Pete and I were wearing our usual clothes
of long-sleeve replica West Perth jumpers and jeans. We had a
good time chatting as we hadn't seen each other for a few
months. Pete's elder brother Mike was nowhere to be seen.

After all the atmosphere and pressure had left the game in
the last quarter, West Perth kicked six goals to three but still
only managed to close the gap to 55 points. WPFC was now in
fifth place, six premiership points adrift of Claremont, and
with two games remaining. Most supporters wrote off the club's
chances of reaching the finals series after this game. The top
five players on the ground were all South Fremantle players,
according to Monday's The West Australian. These included
promising youngsters Wally Matera, Mark Bairstow, and Peter
Sumich (this day at centre-half-back), and the more experienced
hands Craig Edwards (enjoying his life at Fremantle Oval more
than his days as a Royal) and Warren Mosconi (who had made his
league debut as long ago as 1981).

The late Geoff Christian in his match report (full-text
reproduced below) remarked that there was so much young talent
at South Fremantle that aging veterans Benny Vigona and Willie
Roe had played in the reserves. Obviously they hadn't been
needed. Christian made the important observation that while
South had many brilliant individual players on this day it was
their "bulldog spirit" that West Perth just had no hope of
matching anywhere south-west of Leederville Oval. Christian
wrote in his match report as follows: "South had plenty of other
individual stars but it were more the spirit and the team co-
operation revealed by this young Bulldogs' line-up that West
Perth found impossible to match for all but the opening 12
minutes". Neil Winmar (still not yet called "Nicky" by the
press) was mentioned in closing by Christian for his excellent
17-kick, 4-goal effort in the centre which did not even grant
him a spot in his team's best five players. He had been named on
the half-forward flank so even at this young age he was
beginning to show his remarkable versatility. Other good players
for the Southerners were Matt Sambrailo (5.1) at full-forward
and Ross Hutcheson at centre-half-forward. Best players for West
Perth were John Gastev, Craig Nelson, Craig Binder, Les Fong,
Craig Turley, and Corry Bewick. Surprisingly, one of the best
West Perth players in the past three seasons, centre-half-
forward Phil Bradmore, was well held by Peter Sumich. Christian

stated that Sumich was "a first year player who started the season in attack but looked admirably suited at centre-half-back".

South had left its run too late and could not play finals although clearly it was now playing football at finals' standards. By contrast, West Perth showed everybody at the ground that it was far away from being of final round standard even if by good fortune it might just sneak into fourth place. Its recruits were not as good as those at other clubs and its dedication was not what it should have been. The club was relying too much on the heroes of the past few years (such as Phil Bradmore, Les Fong, and Peter Menaglio), and while Corry Bewick had played well all year his advancing age meant he was never going to be anything more than a stopgap. Noel Mugavin was a dependable old warhorse at full-back but he was basically just the last one left standing of the old-guard full-back line which had included at various times Graeme Comerford, Bill Duckworth, John Duckworth, Russell Ellen, Geoff Hendriks, Ray Holden, Ben Jager, and Mick O'Brien.

The club had failed to recruit strong new key attacking players (to replace Rod Alderton and Brian Adamson and in time Phil Bradmore) nor had it recruited new key defenders (to replace Graeme Comerford, John Duckworth, Geoff Hendriks, Ray Holden, and Noel Mugavin). The fact that the ex-West Perth player Mick Rea had morphed into an excellent full-forward at Perth and was leading the goalkicking list with 80 majors after 19 rounds was particularly irksome for West Perth fans. The WPFC coach John Wynne seemed to lack the ability to consistently bring the best out of former second-string players as Mal Brown was now doing at Perth with Mick Rea. Too many good players had been allowed to slip through the net including not only Mick Rea but also David Hart (South Fremantle) and Derek Kickett (Claremont). The juniors coming through were all running midfielders, a type of player West Perth traditionally had an abundance of. West Perth had no tall juniors who could play in key positions coming through whereas South had Craig Edwards, Matt Sambrailo, and Peter Sumich. No West Perth player this day scored more than three goals. (John Gastev kicked 3.2.) In the Round 13 win over Claremont no West Perth player had kicked more than four goals. These statistics tell an important story.

The absence of any West Perth players in the best five players' list shows that on the day it was completely outclassed both as individuals and as a unit. The youngsters at the club were too inconsistent and too easily intimidated at hostile away grounds such as Fremantle Oval. The only young players in West Perth's best six players' list were John Gastev and Craig Turley. Clearly, Dean Laidley (out with an ankle injury) was

sorely missed but I would not be foolish enough to suggest that
his presence might have influenced the result.

Likely line-ups:
(Source: The West Australian, Saturday, 9 August 1986, p. 187)
South Fremantle FC
Backs: Macdonald, Carter, Maskos
Half-backs: D Wilson, Sumich, Mosconi
Centres: B Collard, Bairstow, Lynch
Half-forwards: Winmar, Hutcheson, Todd
Forwards: Bennett, M Sambrailo, D Collard
Ruck: Edwards, Worsfold, Matera
Interchange: Lockhart, Sims
West Perth FC
Backs: Munns, Mugavin, Barns
Half-backs: Binder, Mifka, Turley
Centres: D Bewick, Bell, King
Half-forwards: Menaglio, Bradmore, Lill
Forwards: Waddell, Foley, Gastev
Ruck: Nelson, Fong, C Bewick
Interchange: Collinge, Martin
In: Waddell, Collinge, Martin
Out: Laidley (ankle), Chaplin (ankle), Bennett

Match preview
By David Marsh:
"Today is D-Day – do-or-die – for West Perth, who have their
last chance to stake a claim for a berth in this year's finals.
"And they could not have a tougher assignment, as they meet
giant-killers South Fremantle at Fremantle Oval.
"South have had victories over Subiaco and Perth in the past
three weeks. In addition, West Perth have not won at Fremantle
Oval for eight years".

Match results – Saturday, 9 August, 1986, Fremantle Oval
South Fremantle FC 7.5 16.10 21.12 24.18 (162) d West Perth FC
3.5 6.6 10.9 16.11 (107)
Scorers: SF: Edwards 5.3, Matt Sambrailo 5.1, Winmar 4.2, Matera
4.1, D Collard, Bairstow 2.2, Hutcheson, Todd 1.0, B Collard
0.2, Worsfold, Lockhart 0.1, Forced 0.3.
WP: Gastev 3.2, Bradmore 2.1, Fong, King, D Bewick 2.0, C
Bewick, Collinge 1.2, Foley, C Nelson 1.1, Menaglio, Lill 0.1.
[KJ note: One WP goal seems to be missing from this list.]
(Source: The West Australian, Monday, 11 August 1986, p. 101)

Weather: Fine, light south-westerly breeze.
(Source: The West Australian, Monday, 11 August 1986, p. 101)
Attendance: 5,872 (from WAFL Online)
Free-kicks: SF: 7, 4, 4, 3 - 18.
WP: 4, 5, 4, 1 - 14.

Best players:
WA Footballer of the Year Award:
5 votes Wally Matera (South Fremantle) - A brilliant 22-kick,
four-goal display of roving.
4 votes Mark Bairstow (South Fremantle) - Another strong,
creative performance at centre where he was under notice from
the start.
3 votes Craig Edwards (South Fremantle) - A quality performance
in the ruck and when resting in attack. Marked brilliantly and
kicked four goals.
2 votes Warren Mosconi (South Fremantle) - A dashing and
effective half-back who was outstanding in a solid South
defence.
1 vote Peter Sumich (South Fremantle) - A notable performance at
centre-half-back against Phil Bradmore.
(Source: The West Australian, Monday, 11 August 1986, p. 100)

Team rankings: SF: W Matera 1, M Bairstow 2, C Edwards 3, W
Mosconi 4, P Sumich 5, D Collard 6.
WP: J Gastev 1, C Nelson 2, C Binder 3, L Fong 4, C Turley 5, C
Bewick 6.
(Source: The West Australian, Monday, 11 August 1986, p. 100)

Leading goal-kickers after Round 19 (Top 9 players):
80 - Mick Rea (P)
71 - John Scott (C)
55 - Warren Dean (S), Stephen Sells (S), Colin Waterson (EF)
53 - Brian Peake (EF)
48 - Wayne Ryder (P), Craig Edwards (SF)
41 - Tony Buhagiar (EF)
(Source: The West Australian, Monday, 11 August 1986, p. 101)

Complete match report (full-text):
By the late GEOFF CHRISTIAN:
"South Fremantle are at the start of a bright [new] era in
league football based on an excellent mix of raw talent and
enthusiasm, blended with the right amount of experience.
"That formula was the basis of South's scintillating 55-point
win over West Perth at Fremantle Oval on Saturday, a victory

full of merit and one that should help guarantee that the season
ends a lot happier than it started for the Bulldogs.

"An indication of the amount of ability available at Fremantle
Oval these days can be gauged by the fact that gifted veterans
Benny Vigona and Willie Roe were in action in the reserves on
Saturday.

"The absence of these brilliant attacking players obviously did
not hamper South who kicked their season's highest score [of]
24.18 and almost kicked the Falcons out of business.

"West Perth arrived at Fremantle Oval on Saturday knowing that
victory was a stepping stone into the final four. It was not an
easy task on an oval where the ground surface is obviously a big
advantage for the home team.

"The Falcons left four hours later without even touching that
stepping stone and failed miserably to measure up to the
challenge laid down by South.

"The victory was built around superb performances by No. 1 rover
Wally Matera (their smallest player), ruckman Craig Edwards
(their biggest player) and centreman Mark Bairstow, who fitted
neatly in the middle.

"[Wally] Matera has not given a better display of his roving
skills. His work at the fall of the ball was classical in style
and he made few, if any, handling errors.

"Edwards' marking and general ruck play was superb and the same
could be said of Bairstow whose powerful work in the middle was
of the quality West Perth wished they had available to them.

"South had plenty of other individual stars but it was more the
spirit and the team co-operation revealed by this young
Bulldogs' line-up that West Perth found impossible to match for
all but the opening 12 minutes.

"Everywhere West Perth turned on Saturday they found trouble. On
a day dedicated to national dental health week, West Perth
simply bit off more than they could chew.

They lacked the bite of the Bulldogs; there was [sic] too many
gaps in their play and too many weak spots that obviously were
tender to the probe.

"It was not a day when centre-half-forward Phil Bradmore could
lead the Falcons out of trouble. He was well held by Peter
Sumich, a first year player who started the season in attack but
looked admirably suited at centre-half-back.

"There was plenty of defensive support for Sumich, mainly from
Warren Mosconi, Gavin Carter and Arthur Maskos.

"Things were no better in defence for West Perth.

"Matt Sambrailo, who started the year for South on a wing,
showed natural flair at full-forward when he kicked 5.1 and
Barry Hutcheson has the look of a man who knows how to play at
centre-half-forward.

"And to add to the woes of the West Perth defence, Neil Winmar
[later "Nicky" Winmar] decided to show how well he can play at
centre with a 17-kick, four-goal effort".
(Source: Geoff Christian (1986), "Bulldogs find a formula for
success", The West Australian, Monday, 11 August 1986, p. 100)

APPENDIX C - My West Perth FC all-stars teams
1977-84 best team (compiled in 1984)
Backs: Bill Duckworth, Ray Holden, Ross Gibbs
Half-backs: Ross Prunster, Geoff Hendriks, Shane Fitzsimmons
Centres: Peter Murnane, Mel Whinnen (vice-capt.), Stuart Hiller
Half-forwards: David Palm, Brian Adamson, Barry Day
Forwards: Bill Valli, Rod Alderton, Craig Nelson
Ruck: Ben Jager, Peter Menaglio, Les Fong (capt.)
Interchange: Alan Watling, Dean Warwick, George Michalczyk
Coach: Graham Campbell
Home ground: Leederville Oval!!

1985 best team (compiled in 1985)
Backs: Wayne Dayman, Graeme Comerford, Neale Fong
Half-backs: Brian Perrin, Geoff Hendriks, Dean Laidley
Centres: Peter Murnane, Brendon Bell, Paul Mifka
Half-forwards: Derek Kickett, Phil Bradmore, Les Fong (capt.)
Forwards: Gavin Chaplin, Mark Stephens., Darren Bewick
Ruck: Kim Rogers, Peter Menaglio, Corry Bewick
Interchange: George Michalczyk, John Gastev, John Duckworth
Coach: John Wynne
Home ground: Leederville Oval!!

APPENDIX D - Sandover Medal and Footballer of the Year results, 1984-86

1984 Sandover Medal Count Night, Perth Entertainment Centre

Final Results: Steve Malaxos (Claremont) - 17 votes; Michael Mitchell (Claremont) - 17 votes; Peter Spencer (East Perth) - 17 votes; Laurie Keene (Subiaco) - 14 votes; Peter Menaglio (West Perth) - 14 votes

All West Perth FC vote-getters: Paul Mifka - 9 votes; Brian Perrin - 8 votes; Dean Warwick - 7 votes; Les Fong - 6 votes; Wayne Dayman, Doug Simms - 3 votes; Graeme Comerford, John Gastevich, Derek Kickett, Craig Nelson - 2 votes; Phil Bradmore - 1 vote.

Some media quotes:

"The most disappointing feature of West Perth's voting was that captain Les Fong, who set a consistent standard throughout the year, polled only six votes" - Geoff Christian.

"The umpires' voting reflected the general opinion that West Perth wingman Paul Mifka was the best first-year player in league football" - Geoff Christian.

(Source: Geoff Christian, "Three-Way Tie for the Sandover", The West Australian, Wednesday 29 August 1984, p. 127)

1985 Sandover Medal Count, Golden Ballroom at Sheraton Perth Hotel

Final Results: Murray Wrensted (East Fremantle) - 46 votes; Michael Mitchell (Claremont) - 34 votes; Peter Davidson (Claremont) - 33 votes; Mark Bairstow (South Fremantle) - 33 votes; Dwayne Lamb (Subiaco) - 32 votes; David Bain (East Perth) - 30 votes.

All West Perth FC vote-getters: Dean Laidley - 25 votes (11th place); Kim Rogers - 23 votes (equal 12th place); Gavin Chaplin - 21 votes; Phil Bradmore, Peter Menaglio - 14 votes; Corry Bewick, George Michalczyk - 11 votes; Darren Bewick - 10 votes; John Gastev - 9 votes; Brendon Bell - 6 votes; Graeme Comerford, Doug Simms, Wayne Dayman, Les Fong - 5 votes; Derek Kickett, Peter Cutler, Brian Perrin - 4 votes; Paul Mifka, Dean Warwick - 3 votes; Peter Murnane, Tony Fraser 2 votes.

Team totals (5-4-3-2-1 voting system): East Fremantle 222; West Perth 186; Subiaco 182; Claremont 146; South Fremantle 140; Perth 137; Swan Districts 131; East Perth 116.

(Source: Geoff Christian (1985c), "A birthday Sandover for Wrensted", The West Australian, Tuesday, 27 August, p. 96)

1986 Sandover Medal Count, Golden Ballroom at Sheraton Perth
Hotel
Final Results: Mark Bairstow (South Fremantle) – 39 votes;
Brian Taylor (Subiaco) – 36 votes; Paul Harding (East Fremantle)
– 34 votes; Laurie Keene (Subiaco) – 32 votes; Robert Wiley
(Perth) – 32 votes; Peter Wilson (East Fremantle) – 30 votes.
All West Perth FC vote getters [unbelievably no WP player was in
the Top 24 places]: Les Fong – 14 votes; Dean Laidley, Dan Foley
– 13 votes; John Gastev – 11 votes; Peter Menaglio, Ross Munns,
Brendon Bell – 8 votes; Phil Bradmore, Craig Nelson – 7 votes;
Corry Bewick – 6 votes; Peter Murnane – 4 votes; Kim Rogers,
Simon Lill, Darren Bewick 3 votes; Dean Warwick, Sean King – 2
votes.

Team totals (5-4-3-2-1 voting system): Subiaco 212; East
Fremantle 202; Perth 173; Claremont 158; East Perth 143; South
Fremantle 129; West Perth 128; Swan Districts 115.
(Source: Geoff Christian (1986b), "Bairstow's Sandover in a
count thriller", Tuesday, 16 September, pp. 87-88)

Notes by the author: 1. The Count Night was held in 1986 in the
week prior to the Grand Final rather than in the week prior to
the first semi-final.
2. Although Swan Districts finished eighth out of the then eight
WAFL clubs in 1986, two Swans' players scored more votes than
West Perth's top vote-getter Les Fong. These two players were:
Peter Sartori with 25 votes and Kevin Taylor with 15 votes.
Geoff Christian did not comment about the low number of votes
polled by West Perth players.

1986 WA Footballer of the Year Award
Final Results: Laurie Keene (S) – 45 votes; Paul Harding (EF) –
37 votes; Peter Sartori (37 votes); Mark Bairstow (SF) – 34
votes; R Wiley (P) – 33 votes; P Featherby (S) – 32 votes; B
Peake (EF) – 31 votes; Steve Malaxos (C) – 29 votes; B Taylor
(S) – 28 votes; S Goulding (C) – 24 votes; C Bewick (WP) – 24
votes; W Matera (SF) – 23 votes; C Starcevich (EP) – 22 votes; P
Wilson (EF) – 22 votes; D Panizza (C) – 20 votes; N Taylor (S) –
19 votes; P Bradmore (WP) – 18 votes; M O'Connell (C) – 17
votes; W Dean (S) – 17 votes; A Montgomery (P) – 17 votes; A
Ischenko (EP) – 16 votes; M Watson (P) – 16 votes; D Laidley
(WP) – 16 votes; L Fong (WP) – 25 votes; S Da Rui (EP) – 14
votes; G Neesham (EF) – 14 votes; D Rankin (EF) – 14 votes; M
Mitchell (C) – 13 votes; C Mainwaring (EF) – 13 votes; M
Wrensted (EF) – 13 votes; J Santostefano (P) – 13 votes; D
Holmes (SD) – 13 votes; J Worsfold (SF) – 13 votes; B Cousins

(P) — 12 votes; D Langsford (SD) — 12 votes; D Lamb (S) — 12
votes; B Yorgey (P) — 11 votes; P Mifka (WP) — 11 votes; R
Dennis (EP) — 10 votes; C Edwards (SF) — 10 votes; K Taylor (SD)
— 10 votes.
All remaining West Perth FC vote getters: D Foley — 9 votes; P
Menaglio — 8 votes; S King, C Barnes 6 votes; B Bell, D Warwick
— 5 votes; J Gastev — 4 votes; C Nelson, D Bewick 3 votes; D
Martin 1 vote.
(Source: The West Australian, Monday, 28 August, 1986)

Notes

1. A cheer squad is a semi-organized group of hardcore supporters (typically teenagers) which sits in the same strategic place at home games and which supports the team through chants, songs, flags, and banners. Cheryl Critchley (2010, p. 17) documents that the first Australian Rules cheer squad was formed at VFL/AFL club Richmond in 1959.
2. Brian Atkinson, personal e-mail communication to the author dated 19 November 2011.
3. Brian Atkinson, personal e-mail communication to the author dated 9 December 2010.
4. Personal interview with the author, Kalgoorlie, Western Australia, 14 July 2011.
5. Personal conversation, Perth, 12 July 2011.
6. Personal conversation, Perth, 16 July 2011.
7. The former Heathcote Hospital was used for mental health services from 1929 to 1994.
8. Source: Author's online Facebook conversation with Andrew Mulcahy, 24 April 2018.
9. Personal interview, 14 July 2011.
10. Two pictures of Fat Pam's WPFC cheer squad at East Fremantle Oval on 8 August 1981 can be viewed at the following link: http://waflgoldenera.blogspot.com/2013/12/picture-gallery-fat-pams-west-perth.html [accessed 5 December 2013].
11. As at 26 December 2016.
12. As at 26 December 2016.
13. Brian Atkinson, personal e-mail communication to the author dated 19 November 2011.
14. Melbourne Knights' supporter, personal e-mail communication to the author dated 23 August 2010.
15. Ron (Ronald Brian) Davis (DOB 11/8/1963) played 13 senior games for West Perth in 1984-85 and kicked 22 goals.
16. Group interview, 11 January 2011.
17. Source: Personal Facebook communication with Ben McA., 5 October 2017.
18. Source: My personal notes compiled during the 1984 season.
19. Brian Atkinson, personal e-mail communication to the author dated 19 November 2011.
20. Personal Interview, 8 July 2011.
21. Personal interview, 14 July 2011.
22. Personal interview, 14 July 2011.
23. Brian Atkinson, personal interview, 8 July 2011.
24. Brian Atkinson, personal interview, 8 July 2011.